About the Series

It might almost be said that the most enchanting part of baseball lies not in watching it, but in remembering it. No sport lends itself so effortlessly to memory, to conversation; no sport has so graphic an afterlife in its statistics; nor has any been photographed so thoroughly and excitingly.

Beginning with 1901, the year most historians identify as the dawn of baseball's "modern era," there have been nearly 90 seasons, with no two even remotely alike. The mention of a certain year can evoke the memory of a team, the image of a man, or the drama of a moment. For many fans, it is all so vivid that baseball has become for them a long calendar of historical events.

Every season begins the same, with everyone equal on Opening Day, stirring with optimism and anticipation. And every season ends the same way, with surprises and disappointments, among teams and individuals both. No baseball summer has even been, or can be, dull. No baseball summer has ever been forgotten, for every one has been a source of stories and numbers, many of which have become part of our national folklore.

It is the purpose of this series of books to make it all happen one more time.

The Bantam
Baseball Collection

#1

1959
The Year
That Was

Written by
Donald Honig

Packaged by Angel Entertainment, Inc.
and M.I.B. Baseball Enterprises, Inc.

BANTAM BOOKS
TORONTO • NEW YORK • LONDON • SYDNEY • AUCKLAND

1959 The Year That Was

A Bantam Book / April 1989

Bantam Books are published by Bantam Books, a division of Bantam Doubleday Dell Publishing
Group, Inc. Its trademark, consisting of the words "Bantam Books" and the portrayal of a rooster, is
Registered in U.S. Patent and Trademark Office and in other countries. Marca Registrada, Bantam
Books, 666 Fifth Avenue, New York, New York, 10103.

PRINTED IN THE UNITED STATES OF AMERICA

0 9 8 7 6 5 4 3 2 1

Contents

Introduction

In 1959, the eight years of President Dwight D. Eisenhower were coming to a close. Noted in retrospect for its comparative tranquility, the Eisenhower era was closing with some ominous rumblings. In January, Fidel Castro had completely taken over the government of Cuba and was busy assuring United States political leaders that "we are not Communists." In August, Communist North Vietnamese troops began massing for an attack on neighboring Laos. Also in August, there were violent protests in Little Rock, Arkansas, as black students began integrating that city's Central High School.

Castro soon proved himself to be a liar, and one of the minor offshoots of the hardening antagonism between Cuba and the United States was the Cuban dictator's prohibition on Cuban ballplayers playing in the United States (among major league stars were the Havana-born Minnie Miñoso and Camilo Pascual).

An ironic counterpoint to the turmoil in Little Rock was the complete integration of all big-league clubs, achieved that year when the Boston Red Sox added infielder Pumpsie Green to their roster. (The Red Sox had been the only club never to have a black player.) Providing additional contrast to the disturbances in Little Rock was the fact that blacks had for years been playing on minor-league teams all over the South, without any notable racial incidents.

So, in 1959, baseball, normally isolated within its own unique universe, felt itself brushed by international events and at the same time, the sport continued to make its quiet contributions to a burgeoning civil rights movement.

1

In the ball park itself, the year was characterized by the unexpected: not only did the Yankees not win (for only the second time in 11 years), but the club that toppled them in the American League was the Chicago White Sox (for the first time in 40 years). In the National League, the winners were the recently transplanted Los Angeles Dodgers, recovering from a seventh-place finish the year before. And the Dodgers' victory brought the World Series to the West Coast for the very first time.

It was 1959—the year that was...

The National League Pennant Race

When the Dodgers took their transcontinental hop from Brooklyn to Los Angeles in 1958, they were a club that had won four pennants in six years, a club filled with glittering star names. However, the reality was that many of those names were on the down side of their careers: former Ebbets Field heroes like Duke Snider, Carl Furillo, Pee Wee Reese, Gil Hodges, Don Newcombe and Carl Erskine had seen their greatest years in Brooklyn. So the Dodgers free-fell through the league in 1958, all the way to seventh place.

Some people attributed the Dodgers' decline to an inability to make the adjustment from Brooklyn to Los Angeles (admittedly a cultural difference of harrowing dimensions). Others said it was the difficulties inherent in playing in the Los Angeles Coliseum, a singularly bizarre ball park featuring a left field barrier that was positively intimate with home plate (251 feet down the line) and right and center fields that shot out toward the horizon.

"People said that the ball park was so weird it was impossible to win there," Dodger manager Walter Alston said. "Well, I don't know about that, but I do know that somebody was winning in the Coliseum, because we were losing a lot of games there in 1958."

Consequently, a lot of people were surprised when a year later the Dodgers, as abruptly as they had descended, rode the elevator back to the top. They won the National League pennant in a best two-of-three playoff against the Milwaukee Braves, with whom they had finished the regular season in a tie, each club with an 86-68 record.

3

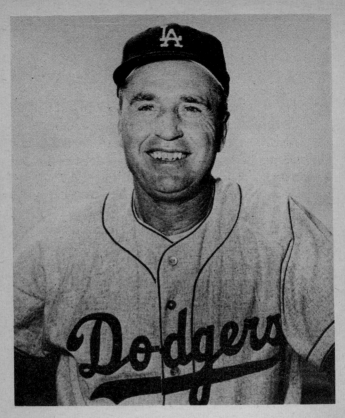

Los Angeles Dodger manager Walter Alston. He managed the Dodgers for 23 years (1954-1976), winning seven pennants. His big-league playing career consisted of one at-bat with the Cardinals (in 1936). He struck out.

"We hardly tore the league apart," Alston said, "but we won. You know, when we finished seventh in 1958, we won 71 games—we were only five games away from fourth place—so it wasn't as horrendous as it seemed. I can remember when the Dodgers won 104 games in 1942 and finished second. So I was happy with what we did in 1959. It's not how many games you win, but how many do you need for the pennant. We won as many as we had to win, which is what I'll take every year."

The 1959 National League pennant race was a three-cornered dance between the Dodgers, Braves and San Francisco Giants, close enough to go into the season's final day with the possibility of a three-way tie. In order for this unprecedented situation to occur, the Giants would have had to win their doubleheader while the Braves and Dodgers were losing their games. It didn't happen: the Giants lost their doubleheader, while the Braves and Dodgers each won their games.

Fred Haney's Braves had begun the season as heavy favorites to take their third straight pennant. In its annual spring poll of the Baseball Writers Association, *The Sporting News* found 147 out of the 226 respondents picking the Braves, while 36 favored the Pittsburgh Pirates and 34 the Giants. The Dodgers were picked by only two writers.

With an 11-6 April, the Dodgers got off to the best start in the league, but then stumbled to 14-17 in May, enabling the Braves to grab the top rung. Haney's club remained in first place until early July, with the Dodgers and Giants slogging along behind them, playing just well enough to remain in contention. The Braves were never more than 4½ games in front.

In early July, Bill Rigney's Giants dislodged the Braves at the top and remained there for the next ten weeks (except for two days). No one was able to break things open: in July and August the Giants were 30-25, the Braves 28-29, the Dodgers 29-24. Except for a brief look-see in April, the

Dodgers were never in first place until the competitive temperatures began to rise in mid-September.

Beginning on September 19, the lead changed hands on seven of the next nine days. A five-game losing streak gradually let the air out of the Giants' balloon and the final day of the regular season found the Dodgers and Braves in a tie. For the Dodgers, it was the fifth time in 11 years that they were involved in a pennant race that ran to the schedule's concluding game. On that day, the Dodgers' Roger Craig beat the Cubs, 7-1, in Chicago, while the Braves' Bob Buhl beat the Phillies, 5-2, at Milwaukee. This forced a playoff, the third in National League history, the Cardinals having beaten the Dodgers in 1946 and the Giants having beaten the Dodgers in 1951. (National League rules at the time called for the two-of-three format, while in the American League it was a one-game sudden-death shootout.)

The first playoff game was played on Monday, September 28, at Milwaukee's County Stadium. The starters were left-hander Danny McDevitt for the Dodgers and Carlton Willey for the Braves. The Dodgers took a one-run lead in the top of the first. Then the Braves struck for two in the bottom of the second, and Alston pulled out McDevitt and brought in his ace reliever Larry Sherry.

"Was it unorthodox to bring in my best relief pitcher in the second inning?" Alston asked. "Well, I was fighting for a pennant and there were no more tomorrows." In effect, he was saying that the strategies of April and May often bear little resemblance to those of September and October; it was strictly an apples-and-oranges comparison. And skilled manager that he was, Alston knew the difference: do the orthodox in spring and summer and you might have the chance to do the unorthodox in autumn.

Larry Sherry. He began the season in the minors and ended it as a World Series hero.

Sherry pitched brilliantly, shutting down the Braves on four hits and no runs for the final 7²/₃ innings. The Dodgers tied the score in the top of the third. Then, in the top of the sixth, catcher John Roseboro hit a home run to give Los Angeles a 3-2 lead, and that was the final score.

The teams flew to Los Angeles that night and played

7

Gil Hodges. When they talked about the strongest men in baseball, his name was always mentioned.

the second game the next afternoon in the Coliseum. With 21-game winner Lew Burdette starting for the Braves against Don Drysdale (17-13), the visitors pecked away and took a 5-2 lead in the bottom of the ninth.

Burdette had allowed no Dodger base runner past first

base since Charlie Neal's leadoff homer in the bottom of the fourth. Then, in the bottom of the ninth with nobody out, the Dodgers loaded the bases on singles by Wally Moon, Duke Snider and Gil Hodges. Don McMahon replaced Burdette and was greeted with a two-run single by Norm Larker, sending Hodges to third with the tying run. Haney then brought in Warren Spahn to pitch to the left-handed-hitting Roseboro. Alston countered with Carl Furillo, who pinch-hit a sacrifice fly, tying the score.

The game then went into extra innings, with Joey Jay on the mound for the Braves and Stan Williams for the Dodgers. The two right-handers maintained the deadlock through the tenth and eleventh innings. Williams continued firing hitless, shutout ball through the top of the twelfth.

With Bob Rush on the mound for the Braves in the bottom of the twelfth, the Dodgers, with two out and nobody on base, suddenly struck. Hodges walked and Joe Pignatano singled him to second. Furillo then hit a high bounder that Felix Mantilla (filling in at short for an injured Johnny Logan) grabbed behind second base. Making a hurried, off-balance throw, Mantilla bounced the ball in front of first baseman Frank Torre. The ball skidded past Torre as Hodges wheeled around third and came home with the run, completing a remarkable leap for the team—from seventh place to the World Series in one year.

The National League Teams That Year

Los Angeles Dodgers

There was no comparison between the 1959 pennant-winning Los Angeles Dodgers and the Dodger clubs that had dominated the league just a few years before in Ebbets Field. Where the Brooklyn teams had used a heavy-hitting attack to bludgeon their opponents, Walter Alston's winners in 1959 (and later, in 1963, 1965, 1966) finessed the opposition with timely hitting, speed afoot and strong pitching.

There were also no stellar individual performances on the 1959 team. The thirty-five-year-old Hodges led the team with 25 home runs, drove in 80 runs and batted .276. Snider hit 23 homers and led the club with 88 RBIs and a .308 average. Overall, the team hit 148 home runs, fifth best in the eight-team league, while the club batting average of .257 was bettered by five other teams.

Thus, there was nothing spectacular about the 1959 Dodgers, as their 86 regular-season wins attest. Their longest winning streak during the season was seven games; but during the ever-tightening September vise, they won 13 of their last 18, plus the two playoff victories. As far as personnel was concerned, the team pretty much resembled the squad that had finished seventh the year before. There were a number of significant changes, however, some of them not coming to pass until mid-season.

The most crucial off-season acquisition was that of outfielder Wally Moon, obtained from the Cardinals in exchange for outfielder Gino Cimoli. Moon gave the club a solid season, batting .302 and hitting 19 home runs. A left-handed hitter, Wally had a knack of stroking balls over the neighborly screen in left, blows that were inevitably called "Moon Shots."

On June 1, the club brought shortstop Maury Wills up from the minors. Described by Alston as "one of the key players," Wills replaced Don Zimmer at the position and breathed new life into the team. (Zimmer batted just .165 for the season.) Wills batted little more than .200 until the September crush, and then went on a .429 tear through the team's last 17 games and ended up at .260.

In discussing Wills, Alston said, "You know, outside of his legs, he was not born with the greatest natural abilities. He had a pretty good arm, but he had to learn to play shortstop. He had to learn to field a ground ball. He became an excellent bunter and, with the help of Bobby Bragan, one of our minor-league managers, a switch-hitter. He was a man of tremendous determination and ambition—always working hard, trying to improve."

The team got workmanlike seasons from second baseman Charlie Neal (.287) and thirdbaseman Jim Gilliam (.282). A most versatile performer, Gilliam (singled out by Alston as a particularly good "team player") could play second, third and the outfield with equal skill. The regular catcher was Johnny Roseboro, who had joined the team in Brooklyn in 1957 and who would one day become the last Brooklyn Dodger to play for the Los Angeles contingent.

Alston's outfield consisted of Moon, Snider and Don Demeter. Demeter, a rangy youngster who came out of the farm system, had some good years in the majors but never quite became the consistent long-ball hitter the team hoped he would.

The Dodger bench strength included young Ron Fairly, who was at the beginning of a 20-year career, and Norm

Larker, who filled in at first and the outfield and batted .289. Joe Pignatano was the backup catcher behind Roseboro.

On the mound, the ace was twenty-two-year-old Don Drysdale, already in his fourth Dodger season. For Drysdale,

Don Drysdale, L.A.'s top winner in 1959. He liked to pitch inside, his attitude being, "If you're standing where I'm pitching, it isn't my fault."

13

who had been 12-13 in 1958, it was a turnaround year. According to Alston, Drysdale, who liked to work inside to right-handed hitters, had been intimidated by the nearness of that left field screen and consequently altered his style of pitching. In 1959, however, he returned to his normal pitching tactics and turned in a 17-13 record, including nine of ten from mid-June to early August. The big right-hander also led the league with 242 strikeouts, helping the staff to a then-record 1,077 strikeouts. He also pitched four shutouts, good enough to tie him with six other pitchers for the league lead.

Behind Drysdale was lefty Johnny Podres, hero of the 1955 World Series, with a 14-9 mark. The next big winner was right-hander Roger Craig, with an 11-5 record. Craig had been with the club in Brooklyn, suffered an arm injury in Los Angeles and had been sent back to the minors. He was recalled from Spokane in the Pacific Coast League on June 19 and went on to rack up his 11 wins (including four shutouts) in little more than half a season. Craig's 2.06 ERA was the league's lowest, but the tall right-hander fell $1\frac{2}{3}$ innings short of the requisite 154 innings pitched needed to qualify for the title.

Slowly beginning to round into the form that would one day see him become the greatest pitcher of his time was twenty-three-year-old left-hander Sandy Koufax. For years, his speed and his wildness had made him a source of both elation and despair to his employers. But now hard work and relentless determination were beginning to put a fine edge on his talents. In 1959, Koufax was just 8-6, but had 173 strikeouts in 153 innings and lowered his bases on balls significantly.

With their long-time relief ace Clem Labine beginning to lose some of the bite on the sinker that had made him a bullpen star in Brooklyn, the Dodgers once more reached

Maury Wills came up during the middle of the 1959 season and hit .260. Three years later, he shattered all records by stealing 104 bases.

down to Spokane and brought up reliever Larry Sherry. The hard-throwing right-hander stabilized the bullpen, turning in a 7-2 record. "He made a hell of a difference," Alston said succinctly.

Rounding out the club's starters were lefty Danny McDevitt (10-8) and right-hander Stan Williams (5-5).

The Dodgers led the league in stolen bases with 84, which by latter-day standards is merely a one-man total. Maury Wills, who in 1962 would begin the stolen base revolution, swiped just seven bases in his half-season.

NAME	G by POS	B	AGE	G	AB	R	H	2B	3B	HR	RBI	BB	SO	SB	BA	SA
LOS ANGELES 1st 88–68 .564				WALT ALSTON (Defeated Milwaukee in playoff 2 games to 0)												
TOTALS			28	156	5282	705	1360	196	46	148	667	591	891	84	.257	.396
Gil Hodges	1B113, 3B4	R	35	124	413	57	114	19	2	25	80	58	92	3	.276	.513
Charlie Neal	2B151, SS1	R	28	151	616	103	177	30	11	19	83	43	86	17	.287	.464
Don Zimmer	SS88, 3B5, 2B1	R	28	97	249	21	41	7	1	4	28	37	56	-3	.165	.249
Jim Gilliam	3B132, 2B8, OF4	B	30	145	553	91	158	18	4	3	34	96	25	23	.282	.345
Duke Snider	OF107	L	32	126	370	59	114	11	2	23	88	58	71	1	.308	.535
Don Demeter	OF124	R	24	139	371	55	95	11	1	18	70	16	87	5	.256	.437
Wally Moon	OF143, 1B1	L	29	145	543	93	164	26	11	19	74	81	64	15	.302	.495
Johnny Roseboro	C117	L	26	118	397	39	92	14	7	10	38	52	69	7	.232	.378
Ron Fairly	OF88	L	20	118	244	27	58	12	1	4	23	31	29	0	.238	.344
Norm Larker	1B55, OF30	L	28	106	311	37	90	14	1	8	49	26	25	0	.289	.418
Maury Wills	SS82	B	26	83	242	27	63	5	2	0	7	13	27	7	.260	.298
Rip Repulski	OF31	R	31	53	94	11	24	4	0	2	14	13	23	0	.255	.362
Joe Pignatano	C49	R	29	52	139	17	33	4	1	1	11	21	15	1	.237	.302
Carl Furillo	OF25	R	37	50	93	8	27	4	0	0	13	7	11	0	.290	.333
Don Drysdale	P44	R	22	46	91	9	15	1	1	4	12	4	31	0	.165	.330
Bob Lillis	SS20	R	29	30	48	7	11	2	0	0	2	3	4	0	.229	.271
2 Chuck Essegian	OF10	R	27	24	46	6	14	6	0	1	5	4	11	0	.304	.500
1 Dick Gray	3B11	R	27	21	52	8	8	1	0	2	4	6	12	0	.154	.288
1 Jim Baxes	3B10	R	30	11	33	4	10	1	0	2	5	4	7	1	.303	.515
Frank Howard	OF6	R	22	9	21	2	3	0	1	1	6	2	9	0	.143	.381
1 Solly Drake	OF4	B	28	9	8	2	2	0	0	0	0	1	3	1	.250	.250
Sandy Amoros 29 L 1-5, Norm Sherry 27 R 1-3, Tommy Davis 20 R 0-1																

Numbers next to a player's name indicate that he played for more than one team during the season.

NAME	T	AGE	W	L	PCT	SV	G	GS	CG	IP	H	BB	SO	ShO	ERA
		27	88	68	.564	26	156	156	43	1412	1317	614	1077	14	3.79
Don Drysdale	R	22	17	13	.567	2	44	36	15	271	237	93	242	4	3.45
Johnny Podres	L	26	14	9	.609	0	34	29	6	195	192	74	145	2	4.11
Roger Craig	R	28	11	5	.688	0	29	17	7	163	122	45	76	4	2.06
Danny McDevitt	L	26	10	8	.556	4	39	22	6	145	149	51	106	2	3.97
Sandy Koufax	L	23	8	6	.571	2	35	23	6	153	136	92	173	1	4.06
Larry Sherry	R	23	7	2	.778	3	23	9	1	94	75	43	72	1	2.20
Stan Williams	R	22	5	5	.500	0	35	15	2	125	102	86	89	0	3.96
Clem Labine	R	32	5	10	.333	9	56	0	0	85	91	25	37	0	3.92
Johnny Klippstein	R	31	4	0	1.000	2	28	0	0	46	48	33	30	0	5.87
Chuck Churn	R	29	3	2	.600	1	14	0	0	31	28	10	24	0	4.94
Art Fowler	R	36	3	4	.429	2	36	0	0	61	70	23	47	0	5.31
Gene Snyder	L	28	1	1	.500	0	11	2	0	26	32	20	20	0	5.54
Carl Erskine	R	32	0	3	.000	1	10	3	0	23	33	13	15	0	7.83
Fred Kipp	L	27	0	0	.000	0	2	0	0	3	2	3	1	0	0.00
Bill Harris	R	27	0	0	.000	0	1	0	0	2	0	1	0	0	0.00

Milwaukee Braves

The Braves were considered by many to be the strongest club in the National League in 1959 and, indeed, their roster included three of the most notable players of the postwar era: outfielder Henry Aaron, thirdbaseman Eddie Mathews, and left-hander Warren Spahn. In addition to these man-sized talents, there were first-baseman Joe Adcock, shortstop Johnny Logan, catcher Del Crandall, outfielders Wes Covington and Bill Bruton, and pitchers Lew Burdette and Bob Buhl.

Aaron, in the full ripeness of his brilliant career, turned in one of his most productive seasons. The quiet Alabaman with the quick wrists led the league with a .355 batting average (highest of his career) and with 223 hits; he also hit 46 doubles, 39 home runs, and drove in 123 runs.

"Sometimes I'd sit around with Joe McCarthy," Braves manager Fred Haney said, referring to the old Yankee manager, "and listen to him reminisce. He'd talk about Gehrig and DiMaggio, saying what great players they were and how little trouble they gave him. They were quiet, never temperamental, and dedicated to the team. Well, that's exactly how Hank Aaron was."

Eddie Mathews was the league's home run leader with 46 (the Braves' total of 177 homers was more than that of any other National League club). Going into the playoff with the Dodgers, Mathews had been tied with the Cubs' Ernie Banks at 45 apiece, but then hit one in the second playoff game (everything that happens in these games counts in the season's records). It was the fourth 40-home-run season in the last seven years for Mathews, who was establishing power-hitting

Milwaukee catcher Del Crandall.   L.

It was a fairly routine year for Henry Aaron in 1959—39 home runs, 123 runs batted in.   R.

records for thirdbasemen that would eventually be broken by Mike Schmidt in the 1980s. Eddie also batted .306 and drove in 114 runs, fifth best in the league.

The third big slugger on the Milwaukee club was Joe Adcock, who hit 25 home runs, despite playing in just 115 games. Adcock shared first base with the slick-fielding Frank Torre, who batted just .228. (Frank was the older brother of Joe Torre, future National League MVP and later manager of the New York Mets and Atlanta Braves.)

The Braves sorely missed the talents of their veteran secondbaseman Red Schoendienst, who had been hospitalized with tuberculosis the previous fall and forced to sit out virtually the entire 1959 season. The difficulties in replacing

Eddie Mathews. According to his manager Fred Haney, "Eddie was the best guy to have on your side when a brawl broke out. He could hit like a heavyweight." Eddie also hit like a heavyweight at home plate: 512 career home runs.

Schoendienst were apparent when, at one time or another during the season, the club ran seven other players out to play the position. Felix Mantilla played 60 games at second, batting just .215; American League veteran Bobby Avila got into 51 games and batted .238; Johnny O'Brien appeared in 37 games and batted .198. The second base position was a season-long headache that resisted all medication applied to it.

Warren Spahn, Milwaukee's smooth and tireless left-hander. No "wrongsider" ever won more in a career: 363.

Shortstop Johnny Logan batted .291, the second-best average of his career. Center-fielder Bill Bruton batted .289 and stole 13 bases, nearly one third of the team's total. Power-

Lew Burdette. Accusations that he threw a wet one were so frequent and so vehement that you expected to see them lay a tarpaulin on the mound when he pitched.

hitting outfielder Wes Covington missed the final six weeks of the season after tearing ligaments in his knee, leaving his

.279 average frozen. Wes, however, had been a disappointment in the big-bang department, hitting just seven home runs in his 373 at bats, compared to the 24 he hit in 294 at-bats in 1958.

Behind the plate, the Braves had one of the best in Del Crandall, at the age of twenty-nine already a nine-year veteran (not counting two years in military service). Crandall batted .272, hit 18 home runs, and for the second year in a row led league catchers in fielding (.994).

With disappointing years from right-handers Joey Jay (6-11) and Carlton Willey (5-9), and with Bob Buhl (15-9) missing almost a month in mid-season with arm miseries, the burden fell on Warren Spahn and Lew Burdette. The two veterans responded admirably, each posting 21-15 records (for Spahn, it was his tenth season as a 20-game winner). Each of the aces had four shutouts, tying them for the league lead with five other pitchers. Burdette's 39 starts were the most in the league, while Spahn led with 21 complete games in 36 starts.

Outfielder Frank Howard broke into a few games for the Dodgers during the 1959 season. At 6'7" and around 260 pounds, the young man was an impressive sight. One morning, a Los Angeles newspaperman encountered Dodgers manager Walter Alston in the lobby of the hotel where the club was staying.

"I just had breakfast with Howard," the writer said, "and I can't believe it."

"Can't believe what?" Alston asked.

"He had bacon, sausages, eggs, toast, muffins, coffee, two infielders and a pitcher."

NAME	G by POS	B	AGE	G	AB	R	H	2B	3B	HR	RBI	BB	SO	SB	BA	SA
MILWAUKEE 2nd 86–70 .551 2				FRED HANEY (Defeated by Los Angeles in playoff 2 games to 0)												
TOTALS			29	157	6388	724	1426	216	36	177	683	488	765	41	.265	.417
Joe Adcock	1B89, OF21	R	31	115	404	53	118	19	2	25	76	32	77	0	.292	.535
Felix Mantilla	2B60, SS23, 3B9, OF7	R	24	103	251	26	54	5	0	3	19	16	31	6	.215	.271
Johnny Logan	SS138	R	32	138	470	59	137	17	0	13	50	57	45	1	.291	.411
Eddie Matthews	3B148	L	27	148	594	118	182	16	8	46	114	80	71	2	.306	.593
Hank Aaron	OF152, 3B5	R	25	154	629	116	223	46	7	39	123	51	54	8	.355	.636
Bill Bruton	OF133	L	33	133	478	72	138	22	6	6	41	35	54	13	.289	.397
Wes Covington (KJ)	OF94	L	27	103	373	38	104	17	3	7	45	26	41	0	.279	.397
Del Crandall	C146	R	29	150	518	65	133	19	2	21	72	46	48	5	.257	.423
Frank Torre	1B87	L	27	115	263	23	80	15	1	1	33	35	12	0	.228	.304
Mickey Vernon	1B10, OF4	L	41	74	91	8	20	4	0	3	14	7	20	0	.220	.363
Andy Pafko	OF64	R	38	71	142	17	31	8	2	1	15	14	15	0	.218	.324
3 Bobby Avila	2B51	R	35	51	172	29	41	3	2	3	19	24	31	3	.238	.331
Lee Maye	OF44	L	24	51	140	17	42	5	1	4	16	7	26	2	.300	.436
Johnny O'Brien	2B37	R	28	44	116	16	23	4	0	1	8	11	15	0	.198	.259
Stan Lopata	C11, 1B2	R	33	25	48	0	5	0	0	0	4	3	13	0	.104	.104
Casey Wise	2B20, SS5	B	26	22	76	11	13	2	0	1	5	10	5	0	.171	.237
Mel Roach (KJ)	2B8, OF4, 3B1	R	26	18	31	1	3	0	0	0	0	2	4	0	.097	.097
Del Rice (BL)	C8	R	36	13	29	3	6	0	0	0	1	2	3	0	.207	.207
1 Joe Morgan	2B7	L	28	13	23	2	5	1	0	0	1	2	4	0	.217	.261
3 Ray Boone	1B3	R	35	13	15	3	3	0	0	1	2	4	2	0	.200	.400
Enos Slaughter	OF6	L	43	11	18	0	3	0	0	0	1	3	3	0	.167	.167
Chuck Cottier	2B10	R	23	10	24	1	3	1	0	0	1	3	7	0	.125	.167
1 Jim Pisoni	OF9	R	29	9	24	4	4	1	0	0	0	2	6	0	.167	.208
Al Spengler	OF4	L	25	6	12	3	5	1	0	1	0	1	1	1	.417	.583
John DeMerit 23 R 1-5, Red Schoendienst (IL) 36 B 0-3																

NAME	T	AGE	W	L	PCT	SV	G	GS	CG	IP	H	BB	SO	ShO	ERA
		29	86	70	.551	18	157	157	69	1401	1406	429	775	18	3.51
Lew Burdette	R	32	21	15	.583	1	41	30	20	290	312	38	105	4	4.07
Warren Spahn	L	38	21	15	.583	0	40	36	21	292	282	70	143	4	2.96
Bob Buhl (SA)	R	30	15	9	.625	0	31	24	12	198	181	74	105	4	2.86
Juan Pizarro	L	22	6	2	.750	0	29	14	6	134	117	70	126	2	3.76
Joey Jay	R	23	6	11	.353	0	34	19	4	136	130	64	88	1	4.10
Don McMahon	R	29	5	3	.625	15	60	0	0	81	81	37	55	0	2.56
Bob Rush	R	33	5	6	.455	0	31	9	1	101	102	23	64	1	2.41
Carl Willey	R	28	5	8	.357	0	26	15	5	117	126	31	51	2	4.15
Bob Trowbridge	R	29	1	0	1.000	1	16	0	0	30	45	10	22	0	6.00
Bob Giggie	R	25	1	0	1.000	0	13	0	0	20	24	10	15	0	4.05
Bob Hartman	L	21	0	0	.000	0	3	0	0	2	6	2	1	0	22.50

San Francisco Giants

Bill Rigney was managing the Giants when they left New York in 1957. Still with the club in 1959, the bespectacled former infielder came close to leading the transplanted New Yorkers to the pennant. A September slump—they lost 11 of their last 16—cost the Giants dearly. The problem was a batting slump and, more seriously, tired arms on the pitching staff.

Rigney had pretty much relied on four starters all season—Sam Jones, Jack Sanford, and left-handers Johnny Antonelli and Mike McCormick. Together, they started 135 of the team's 154 games. In addition, Jones, who was 21-15, relieved 15 times. The big right-hander, whose sidearm delivery intimidated many right-handed batters, was the league's ERA leader with 2.82, and along with Antonelli (19-10) had four shutouts, tying for the league lead. Sanford was 15-12 and McCormick 12-16. Slow-baller Stu Miller was the number-one reliever.

Despite what was for much of the season a strong starting rotation, the Giants were unable to put on a sustained drive, never winning more than four in a row during the season.

The team's batting attack was led by Willie Mays and Orlando Cepeda, who were joined at the end of July by rookie Willie McCovey. McCovey's debut was memorable—two singles and two triples in four at bats against the Phillies' Robin Roberts. Despite getting into just 52 games, McCovey, who batted .354 and hit 13 home runs, was voted the league's Rookie of the Year. The youngster's success, however, gradually created a problem for the team. The question was, who to

Sam Jones. His sidearm curve was a nightmare for right-handed hitters. He led the National League in strikeouts three times.

Willie Mays: nobody could ever do more on a ball field.

play at first base, McCovey or Cepeda, neither of whom was suited to play anywhere else. Wanting both of these potent bats in the lineup, the club put McCovey in left field; but the big slugger was never very adept out there. Eventually, in 1966, the Giants solved the problem by dealing Cepeda to the Cardinals.

The Giants had Daryl Spencer at second, Eddie Bres-

Orlando Cepeda led the Giants in RBIs (105) and batting average (.351), while hitting 27 homers in 1959.   **L.**

Willie McCovey, 1959's Rookie of the Year in the National League. He went on to become the most-feared hitter in the league.   **R.**

soud at short, and the sharp-fielding Jim Davenport at third. Along with Mays in the outfield were Willie Kirkland (with Mays, Kirkland, and then McCovey in the lineup, sportswriters were able to say the Giants were giving other teams "the Willies") and Jackie Brandt. Mays led the league in stolen bases with 27. The catching was shared by Hobie Landrith and Bob Schmidt.

For the Giants, it was their third and final year in Seals Stadium. This was the modest-sized minor league park they played in while waiting for their permanent home, Candlestick Park, to be built.

NAME	G by POS	B	AGE	G	AB	R	H	2B	3B	HR	RBI	BB	SO	SB	BA	SA
SAN FRANCISCO 3rd 83–71 .5304							BILL RIGNEY									
TOTALS			25	154	5281	705	1377	239	36	167	680	473	875	81	.261	.414
Orlando Capeda	1B122, OF44, 3B4	R	21	151	605	92	192	35	4	27	105	33	100	23	.317	.522
Daryl Spencer	2B151, SS4	R	29	152	555	59	147	20	1	12	62	58	67	5	.265	.369
Ed Bressoud	1B1, 2B1, 3B1, SS1	R	27	104	315	36	79	17	2	9	26	28	55	0	.251	.403
Jim Davenport	3B121, SS1	R	25	123	469	65	121	16	3	6	38	28	65	0	.258	.343
Willie Kirkland	OF117	L	25	126	463	64	128	22	3	22	68	42	84	5	.272	.475
Willie Mays	OF147	R	28	151	575	125	180	43	5	34	104	65	58	27	.313	.583
Jackie Brandt	OF116, 3B18, 1B3, 2B1	R	25	137	429	63	116	16	5	12	57	35	69	11	.270	.415
Hobie Landrith	C109	L	29	109	283	30	71	14	0	3	29	43	23	0	.251	.332
Felipe Alou	OF69	R	24	95	247	38	68	13	2	10	33	17	38	5	.275	.466
Leon Wagner	OF28	L	25	87	129	20	29	4	3	5	22	25	24	0	.225	.419
Andre Rodgers	SS66	R	24	71	228	32	57	12	1	6	24	32	50	2	.250	.390
Bob Schmidt	C70	R	28	71	181	17	44	7	1	5	20	13	24	0	.243	.376
Dusty Rhodes		L	32	54	48	1	9	2	0	0	7	5	9	0	.188	.229
Willie McCovey	1B51	L	21	52	192	32	68	9	5	13	38	22	35	2	.354	.656
Danny O'Connell	3B26, 2B8	R	32	34	58	6	11	3	0	0	0	5	15	0	.190	.241
Jose Pagan	3B18, SS5, 2B3	R	24	31	46	7	8	1	0	0	1	2	8	1	.174	.196
2 Jim Hegan	C21	R	38	21	30	0	4	1	0	0	0	1	10	0	.133	.167
Bob Speake 28 L 1-11, Hank Sauer 40 R 1-15, Roger McCardell 26 R 0-4																

NAME	T	AGE	W	L	PCT	SV	G	GS	CG	IP	H	BB	SO	ShO	ERA
		28	83	71	.539	23	154	154	52	1376	1279	500	873	12	3.47
Sam Jones	R	33	21	15	.583	4	50	35	16	271	232	109	209	4	2.82
Johnny Antonelli	L	29	19	10	.655	1	40	38	17	282	247	76	165	4	3.10
Jack Sanford	R	30	15	12	.556	1	36	31	10	222	198	70	132	0	3.16
Mike McCormick	L	20	12	16	.429	4	47	31	7	226	213	86	151	3	3.98
Stu Miller	R	31	8	7	.533	8	59	9	2	168	164	57	95	0	2.84
Gordon Jones	R	29	3	2	.600	2	31	0	0	44	45	19	29	0	4.30
Al Worthington	R	30	2	3	.400	2	42	3	0	73	68	37	45	0	3.70
Eddie Fisher	R	22	2	6	.250	1	17	5	0	40	57	8	15	0	7.88
Bud Byerly	R	38	1	0	1.000	0	11	0	0	13	11	5	4	0	1.38
Joe Shipley	R	24	0	0	.000	0	10	1	0	18	16	17	11	0	4.50
Dom Zanni	R	27	0	0	.000	0	9	0	0	11	12	8	11	0	6.55
Billy Muffett	R	28	0	0	.000	0	5	0	0	7	11	3	3	0	5.14
Curt Barclay	R	27	0	0	.000	0	1	0	0	0	2	2	0	0	∞
Marshall Renfroe	L	23	0	0	.000	0	1	1	0	2	3	3	3	0	27.00
Ray Monzant (VR) 26															

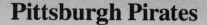

Pittsburgh Pirates

After a strong second-place finish in 1958, Danny Murtaugh's Pirates were expected to contend in 1959. A combination of factors, however, relegated them to fourth place, nine games behind the pennant-winning Dodgers.

"That was a pretty big disappointment to me," Murtaugh said later. "The league wasn't too strong that year. We could've won. We should've won."

While some Pirate players had sub-par years in 1959, reliever Roy Face wasn't one of them. The forkballing little right-hander (he stood approximately 5'8") won 17 consecutive games (he had 22 straight wins over a two-year period) and finished the season with an 18-1 mark. Face's 22 straight wins fell two shy of Carl Hubbell's 1936-37 record, and his 17 wins were two short of Rube Marquard's one-season record, set with the Giants in 1912.

With starter Vern Law going 18-9, the team had two big winners, but after that there was a sharp decline, down to Harvey Haddix's 12-12, Ron Kline's 11-13, and Bob Friend's 8-19. For Friend, the fall-off was particularly precipitous—he had been 22-14 the year before. Another heavy disappointment was right-hander George Witt, who had been 9-2 the year before, his rookie season, closing out with seven straight wins. Witt, however, came down with arm trouble and was 0-7, and what had promised to be a fine major-league career was for all intents and purposes over.

The Pirates had four .290 hitters in the regular lineup—first baseman Dick Stuart (.297), catcher Smoky Burgess (.297), outfielder Roberto Clemente (.296), and third base-

Pittsburgh reliever Elroy Face, who was 18-1 in 1959.

man Don Hoak (.294). Stuart's 27 home runs led the team and so did his 78 runs-batted-in, which was the lowest for a team leader in the league that year.

At second base the Pirates had Bill Mazeroski, by consensus the best-fielding second baseman of his time, and at

Pittsburgh's Bill Mazeroski, generally considered the greatest defensive second baseman of his time.

shortstop was Dick Groat. Along with Clemente, the regular outfielders were Bill Virdon and Bob Skinner. Interestingly, when the Pirates won the world championship one year later, it was with exactly the same team.

NAME	G by POS	B	AGE	G	AB	R	H	2B	3B	HR	RBI	BB	SO	SB	BA	SA
PITTSBURGH 4th 78-78 .506 9							DANNY MURTAUGH									
TOTALS			28	155	5368	651	1414	230	42	112	617	442	715	32	.263	.384
Dick Stuart	1B105, OF1	R	28	118	387	64	118	15	2	27	78	42	86	1	.297	.549
Bill Mazeroski	2B133	R	22	135	493	50	119	15	6	7	59	29	54	1	.241	.339
Dick Groat	SS145	R	28	147	593	74	183	22	7	5	51	32	35	0	.275	.361
Don Hoak	3B155	R	31	155	564	80	166	29	3	8	65	71	75	9	.294	.399
Roberto Clemente (EJ)	OF104	R	24	105	432	80	128	17	7	4	50	15	51	2	.296	.396
Bill Virdon	OF144	L	28	144	519	67	132	24	2	8	41	55	65	7	.254	.355
Bob Skinner	OF142, 1B1	L	27	143	547	78	153	18	4	13	61	67	65	10	.280	.398
Smoky Burgess	C101	L	32	114	377	41	112	28	5	11	59	31	16	0	.297	.485
Rocky Nelson	1B56, OF2	L	34	98	175	31	51	11	0	6	32	23	19	0	.291	.457
Roman Mejias	OF86	R	28	96	276	28	65	6	1	7	28	21	48	1	.236	.341
Dick Schofield	2B28, SS8, OF3	B	24	81	145	21	34	10	1	1	9	16	22	1	.234	.338
1 Ted Kluszewski	1B20	L	34	60	122	11	32	10	1	2	17	5	14	0	.262	.410
Hank Foiles (KJ)	C51	R	30	53	80	10	18	3	0	3	4	7	16	0	.225	.375
Danny Kravitz	C45	L	28	52	162	18	41	9	1	3	21	5	14	0	.253	.377
Harry Bright	OF4, 3B3, 2B1	R	29	40	48	4	12	1	0	3	8	5	10	0	.250	.458

3 Harry Simpson 33 L 4-15, Joe Christopher 23 R 0-12, Ken Hamlin 24 R 1-8, R C Stevens 24 R 2-7, Hardy Peterson 29 R 0-1, Gene Baker (KJ) 34

NAME	T	AGE	W	L	PCT	SV	G	GS	CG	IP	H	BB	SO	ShO	ERA
		28	78	76	.506	17	155	155	48	1393	1432	418	730	7	3.90
Roy Face	R	31	18	1	.847	10	57	0	0	93	91	25	69	0	2.71
Vern Law	R	29	18	9	.667	1	34	33	20	266	245	53	110	2	2.98
Harvey Haddix	L	33	12	12	.500	0	31	29	14	224	189	49	149	2	3.13
Ron Kline	R	27	11	13	.458	0	33	29	7	186	186	70	91	0	4.26
Bob Friend	R	26	8	19	.296	0	35	35	7	235	267	52	104	2	4.02
Bennie Daniels	R	27	7	9	.438	1	34	12	0	101	115	39	67	0	5.44
Ron Blackburn (MS)	R	24	1	1	.500	1	26	0	0	44	50	15	19	0	3.68
Don Gross	L	28	1	1	.500	2	21	0	0	33	28	10	15	0	3.55
13 Bob Porterfield	R	35	1	2	.333	1	36	0	0	41	51	19	19	0	4.39
Freddie Green	L	25	1	2	.333	1	17	1	0	37	37	15	20	0	3.16
George Witt (SA)	R	25	0	7	.000	0	15	11	0	51	58	32	30	0	6.88
1 Bob Smith	L	28	0	0	.000	0	20	0	0	28	32	17	12	0	3.54
Al Jackson	L	23	0	0	.000	0	8	3	0	18	30	8	13	0	6.50
Don Williams	R	27	0	0	.000	0	6	0	0	12	17	3	3	0	6.75
Paul Giel	R	28	0	0	.000	0	4	0	0	8	17	6	3	0	13.50
Dick Hall	R	28	0	0	.000	0	2	1	0	9	12	1	3	0	3.00
Jim Umbricht	R	29	0	0	.000	0	1	1	0	7	7	4	3	0	6.43

Chicago Cubs

With Bob Scheffing at the helm for his third (and final) year, the Cubs finished fifth (tied with Cincinnati) for the second year in a row. They had a 74-80 record, 13 games out of first place. It was their thirteenth straight second-division finish.

However, as late as July 28, Scheffing's team was only 4½ games out of first place. But then a seven-game losing streak began a slide that eventually took them out of the race.

The Chicago offense pretty much began and ended with Ernie Banks. The slugging shortstop hammered his way to his second straight Most Valuable Player Award, becoming the first National Leaguer to earn the distinction two years in a row. Banks hit 45 home runs drove in 143 runs and batted .304. To demonstrate the extreme length of Ernie's shadow in Wrigley Field that year, no other Cub player hit more than 14 homers or knocked in more than 52 runs.

The Cubs had an able player in second baseman Tony Taylor, who batted .280 and tied for second in the league in stolen bases with 23 (the rest of the team had nine among them). At the corners were a couple of players who had seen better days—first baseman Dale Long, who a few years before had set a record by homering in eight straight games for the Pirates; and third baseman Alvin Dark, once upon a time one of the league's top shortstops for the Braves and Giants, but now a thirty-seven-year-old third baseman. George Altman, Lee Walls, Walt Moryn, and former New York Giant hero Bobby Thomson shared the outfield, with Thomson's .259 the best average among them.

The Cubs could score runs, had some power (163 home

Ernie Banks. The Cubs' shortstop was the National League's Most Valuable Player in 1959, as he had been in 1958.   L.

With the Cubs' pitching staff delivering the fewest complete games in the league (30), reliever Don Elston had a busy summer. He and teammate Bill Henry each made 65 appearances, tops in the league.   R.

runs, third best in the league), but they were slow afoot and led the league by striking out 911 times.

Scheffing had one solid starter in right-hander Glen Hobbie, who was 16-13. The only other starter to win in double figures was right-hander Bob Anderson (12-13). The rest of the staff was made up of dubious characters, who provided plenty of work for a pair of fine relievers, Don Elston and lefty Bill Henry, each of whom appeared in a league-high 65 games.

CHICAGO 5th (Tie) 74-80 .481 13 — BOB SCHEFFING

NAME	G by POS	B	AGE	G	AB	R	H	2B	3B	HR	RBI	BB	SO	SB	BA	SA
TOTALS			30	155	5296	673	1321	209	44	163	635	498	911	32	.249	.398
Dale Long	1B85	L	33	110	296	34	70	10	3	14	37	31	53	0	.236	.432
Tony Taylor	2B149, SS2	R	23	150	624	96	175	30	8	8	38	45	86	23	.280	.393
Ernie Banks	SS154	R	28	155	589	97	179	25	6	45	143	64	72	2	.304	.596
Al Dark	3B131, 1B4, SS1	R	37	136	477	80	126	22	9	6	45	55	50	1	.264	.386
Lee Walls	OF119	R	26	120	354	43	91	18	3	8	33	42	73	0	.257	.393
George Altman	OF121	L	26	135	420	54	103	14	4	12	47	34	80	1	.245	.383
Bobby Thomson	OF116	R	35	122	374	55	97	15	2	11	52	35	50	1	.259	.398
Sammy Taylor	C109	L	28	110	353	41	95	13	2	13	43	36	47	1	.269	.428
Walt Moryn	OF104	L	33	117	381	41	89	14	1	14	48	44	68	0	.234	.386
Jim Marshall	1B72, OF8	L	27	108	294	39	74	10	1	11	40	33	39	0	.252	.405
Earl Averill	C32, 3B13, OF5, 2B2	R	27	74	188	22	44	10	0	10	34	15	39	0	.237	.452
2 Irv Noren	OF40, 1B1	L	34	65	158	27	50	6	2	4	19	13	24	2	.321	.482
Cal Neeman	C38	R	30	44	105	7	17	2	0	3	9	11	23	0	.162	.267
Art Schult	1B23, OF15	R	31	42	118	17	32	7	0	2	14	7	14	0	.271	.381
2 Randy Jackson	3B22, OF1	R	33	41	74	7	18	5	1	1	10	11	10	0	.243	.378
Johnny Goryl	2B11, 3B4	R	25	26	48	1	9	3	1	1	6	5	3	1	.188	.354
Billy Williams	OF10	L	21	18	33	0	5	0	1	0	2	1	7	0	.152	.212
Lou Jackson		L	23	8	4	2	1	0	0	0	1	0	2	0	.250	.250

Don Eddy 25 R 0-1, 1 Charlie King 28 R 0-3, Bobby Adams 37 R 0-2, Gordon Massa (MS) 23

NAME	T	AGE	W	L	PCT	SV	G	GS	CG	IP	H	BB	SO	ShO	ERA
		28	74	80	.481	25	155	155	30	1391	1337	519	765	11	4.01
Glen Hobbie	R	23	16	13	.552	0	46	33	10	234	204	106	138	3	3.69
Bob Anderson	R	23	12	13	.480	0	37	36	7	235	245	77	113	1	4.14
Don Elston	R	30	10	8	.556	13	65	0	0	98	77	48	82	0	3.31
Bill Henry	L	31	9	8	.529	12	65	0	0	134	111	48	115	0	2.69
Dave Hillman	R	31	8	11	.421	0	39	24	4	191	178	43	88	1	3.53
Art Ceccarelli	L	29	5	5	.500	0	18	15	4	102	95	37	56	2	4.76
Moe Drabowsky	R	23	5	10	.333	0	31	23	3	142	138	75	70	1	4.12
John Buzhardt	R	22	4	5	.444	0	31	10	1	101	107	28	33	1	4.99
Elmer Singleton	R	41	2	1	.667	0	21	1	0	43	40	12	25	0	2.72
Joe Schaffernoth (EJ)	R	21	1	0	1.000	0	5	1	0	8	11	4	3	0	7.88
Ed Donnelly	R	24	1	1	.500	0	9	0	0	14	18	9	6	0	3.21
Dick Drott (BA)	R	23	1	2	.333	0	8	6	1	27	25	26	15	1	6.00
2 Seth Morehead	L	24	0	1	.000	0	11	2	0	19	26	8	9	0	4.74
1 Taylor Phillips	L	26	0	2	.000	0	7	2	0	17	22	11	5	0	7.41
Ben Johnson	R	28	0	0	.000	0	4	2	0	17	17	4	8	0	2.12
2 Bob Porterfield	R	35	0	0	.000	0	4	0	0	6	14	3	0	0	12.00
Morrie Martin	L	38	0	0	.000	0	3	0	0	2	5	1	1	0	22.50
1 Riverboat Smith	L	31	0	0	.000	0	1	0	0	1	5	2	0	0	54.00

Cincinnati Reds

The heaviest-hitting team in the National League in 1959 finished in a tie for fifth place. The Cincinnati Reds led in batting (.274), slugging (.427), and runs (764), their run total being the second highest in the franchise's history (the 1956 club scored 775 runs). The team received some outstanding individual performances from Frank Robinson, Johnny Temple, Gus Bell and rookie Vada Pinson.

Robinson, who played 125 games at first base that year, batted .311, hit 36 home runs, and drove in 125 runs. Second baseman Temple also batted .311, while outfielders Bell and Pinson batted .293 and .316, respectively. Bell, whose son Buddy was to become a premier third baseman two decades later, drove in 115 runs.

The Reds, however, received a disappointing year from outfielder thirdbaseman Frank Thomas. Acquired during the winter from Pittsburgh, where he had been a top slugger, Thomas labored through a wretched year, batting .225 and hitting just 12 homers, while driving in 47 runs. (With the Pirates the year before, he had hit 35 homers and driven in 109 runs, batting .281.)

The team also suffered when Roy McMillan, arguably the best defensive shortstop in the league, broke a bone in his right hand on June 14 and then fractured a collarbone on August 11. The injuries held McMillan to just 73 games. Replacing him at short was Eddie Kasko, an able man; but no one could sweep the infield like McMillan.

Third base was another problem spot for the Reds that year. With Thomas not hitting, the club made a mid-season

Cincinnati slugger Frank Robinson, the only man ever to be voted MVP in both leagues—with the Reds in 1961 and the Baltimore Orioles in 1966. In 1975, he became baseball's first black manager, taking over the Cleveland Indians.   L.

Gus Bell, one of two outstanding stars in the family, along with his son Buddy, who came to the big leagues eight years after his father had retired.   *R.*

trade for former Phillies "Whiz Kid" Willie Jones. Willie was 33 years old now, no longer a kid, and much of the whiz was gone from his bat, which checked in with a .249 batting average.

Behind the plate, the Reds were sound with Ed Bailey, who caught well and batted .264.

Despite their problems and disappointments, the Reds might have made a run at the top, if their pitching had been of better caliber. Their ace was former Brooklyn Dodger stal-

Johnny Temple, Cincinnati's sparkplug second baseman.

wart Don Newcombe. No longer the fireballer who had daz-zled them in Ebbets Field, big Newk was 13-8, walking just 27 in 222 innings. Always a good hitter, he batted .305, including 5 for 21 as a pinch hitter.

Behind Newcombe was right-hander Bob Purkey (13-18) and then lefty Joe Nuxhall (9-9). Getting into two games apiece were a pair of young southpaws the Reds let get away to greater glory elsewhere—Mike Cuellar and Claude Osteen.

The team's poor first half (35-45) cost manager Mayo Smith his job. Smith, an ebullient character, was replaced by the scowling, no-nonsense Fred Hutchinson. A man of explosive temperament, Hutchinson struck twin chords of fear and respect into his players, one of whom commented, "I saw him almost smile once." Under his leadership, the Reds achieved a record of 39-35 for the second half of the season. In two years, "The Big Bear" would lead the Reds to their first pennant in 21 years.

NAME	G by POS	B	AGE	G	AB	R	H	2B	3B	HR	RBI	BB	SO	SB	BA	SA
CINCINNATI 5th (Tie) 74-80 .481 13				MAYO SMITH 35-45 .438			FRED HUTCHINSON 39-35 .527									
TOTALS			28	154	5288	764	1448	258	34	161	721	499	763	65	.274	.427
Frank Robinson	1B125, OF40	R	23	146	540	106	168	31	4	36	125	69	93	18	.311	.583
Johnny Temple	2B149	R	30	149	598	102	186	35	6	8	67	72	40	14	.311	.430
Eddie Kasko	SS84, 3B31, 2B2	R	27	118	329	39	93	14	1	2	31	14	38	2	.283	.350
3 Willie Jones	3B68	R	33	72	233	33	58	12	1	7	31	28	26	2	.249	.399
Gus Bell	OF145	L	30	148	580	59	170	27	2	19	115	29	44	2	.293	.445
Vada Pinson	OF154	L	20	154	648	131	205	47	9	20	84	55	98	21	.316	.509
Jerry Lynch	OF98	L	28	117	379	49	102	16	3	17	58	29	50	2	.269	.462
Ed Bailey	C117	L	28	121	379	43	100	13	0	12	40	62	53	2	.264	.393
Frank Thames	3B64, OF33, 1B14	R	30	108	374	41	84	18	2	12	47	27	56	0	.225	.380
Roy McMillan (BC)	SS73, OF24	R	28	79	246	38	65	14	2	9	24	27	27	0	.264	.447
Jim Pendleton	3B16, SS3	R	35	65	113	13	29	2	0	3	9	8	18	3	.257	.354
Don Newcombe	P30	L	33	61	105	10	32	2	0	3	21	17	23	0	.305	.410
Dutch Dotterer	C51	R	27	52	161	21	43	7	0	2	17	16	23	0	.267	.348
2 Whitey Lockman	1B20, 2B6, OF1, 3B1	L	32	52	84	10	22	5	1	0	7	4	6	0	.262	.345
Johnny Powers	OF5	L	29	43	8	4	11	2	1	2	4	3	13	0	.256	.488
Pete Whisenant	OF21	R	29	36	71	13	17	2	0	5	11	8	18	0	.239	.479
1 Walt Dropo	1B23	R	36	26	39	4	4	1	0	1	2	4	7	0	.103	.205
Cliff Cook	3B9	R	22	9	21	3	8	2	1	0	5	2	8	1	.381	.571

Bobby Henrich 20 R 0-3, Buddy Gilbert 23 L 3-20, 1 Del Ennis 34 R 4-12, Bob Thurman 42 L 1-4, Don Pavletich 20 R 0-0

NAME	T	AGE	W	L	PCT	SV	G	GS	CG	IP	H	BB	SO	ShO	ERA
		29	74	80	.481	26	154	154	44	1357	1460	456	690	7	4.31
Don Newcombe	R	33	13	8	.619	1	30	29	17	222	216	27	100	2	3.16
Bob Purkey	R	29	13	18	.419	1	38	33	9	218	241	43	78	1	4.25
Joe Nuxhall	L	30	9	9	.500	1	28	21	6	132	155	35	75	1	4.23
2 Jim Brosnan	R	29	8	3	.727	2	26	9	1	83	79	26	56	1	3.36
Brooks Lawrence	R	34	7	12	.368	10	43	14	3	128	144	45	64	0	4.78
Jay Hook	R	22	5	5	.500	0	17	15	4	79	79	39	37	0	5.13
Jim O'Toole	L	22	5	8	.385	0	28	19	3	129	144	73	68	1	5.16
Orlando Pena	R	25	5	9	.357	5	46	8	1	136	150	39	76	0	4.76
Bob Mabe	R	29	4	2	.667	3	18	1	0	30	29	18	8	0	5.40
Willard Schmidt	R	31	3	2	.600	0	36	4	0	71	80	30	40	0	3.93
Luis Arroyo	L	32	1	0	1.000	0	10	0	0	14	17	11	8	0	3.86
Tom Acker	R	29	1	2	.333	2	37	0	0	63	57	37	45	0	4.14
Hal Jeffcoat	R	34	0	1	.000	1	17	0	0	22	21	10	12	0	3.27
Jim Bailey	L	24	0	1	.000	0	3	1	0	12	17	6	7	0	6.00
2 Don Rudolph	L	27	0	0	.000	0	5	0	0	7	13	3	8	0	5.14
Mike Cuellar	L	22	0	0	.000	0	2	0	0	4	7	4	5	0	15.75
Claude Osteen	L	19	0	0	.000	0	2	0	0	8	11	9	3	0	6.75

St. Louis Cardinals

With new manager Solly Hemus calling the shots, the Cardinals got off to a dismal start in 1959, losing 16 of their first 21. They were unable to make a full recovery, despite playing fine ball until the end of July. The team never rose higher than sixth all year, and their seventh-place finish marked only the second time since 1919 that a Cardinal club had fared so poorly.

Symbolizing the team's miserable season was the sudden decline of the veteran Stan Musial. After 16 straight years of hitting over .300—considerably over, generally—the 38-year-old first baseman dropped to .255. In spite of the descent in Musial's usually highly polished batting average, the team's .269 mark was second in the league only to Cincinnati's .274. (That both these teams finished far out of the money pointed up once again one of baseball's cherished axioms, that pitching is "the name of the game.")

Leading the Cardinal attack was outfielder Joe Cunningham, who had a .345 stroke that year, his best ever. Third baseman Ken Boyer batted .309, hit 28 home runs, and drove in 94 runs, while playing a strong third base. The team had a third .300 hitter in outfielder-third baseman Bill White. The former Giant and future broadcaster batted .302.

Second-baseman Don Blasingame batted .289, highest of his career (the Cardinals, however, had Julian Javier coming up and traded Blasingame to the Giants the following December). Shortstop Alex Grammas batted .269, and catcher Hal Smith .270. Outfielder Gino Cimoli, obtained from the Dodgers for Wally Moon, was a .279 hitter in his one-and-only season in St. Louis (the team wanted young

Joe Cunningham, who turned in his best big-league season in 1959, batting .345 for the Cardinals.

Curt Flood, a part-timer in 1959, to start playing regularly). On the bench, the Cardinals had the league's top pinch-hitter (17 hits) in George Crowe, who batted .301.

With reliever Lindy McDaniel tying starter Larry Jackson for the team lead in wins (14), it was obvious that the

Ken Boyer. Dangerous at the plate, brilliant in the field. A lot of people think he belongs in the Hall of Fame.

pitching was in trouble. The third top winner was Vinegar Bend Mizell, a hard-throwing lefty who would one day sit in the United States House of Representatives as a member from North Carolina. The future congressman was 13-10.

Larry Jackson, a steady winner for 14 years.

There was, however, a particularly brilliant sun rising on the Cardinals' horizon that year: rookie right-hander Bob Gibson joined the club in mid-season, broke in with a shutout and went on to a 3-5 record. Gibson later claimed to have an adversarial relationship with Hemus and in fact did not hit his stride until 1961, when Hemus was fired and was replaced by Johnny Keane. At that point, Gibson began showing the form that made him the club's greatest pitcher since Dizzy Dean.

NAME	G by POS	B	AGE	G	AB	R	H	2B	3B	HR	RBI	BB	SO	SB	BA	SA
ST. LOUIS 7th 71-83 .461 16							SOLLY HEMUS									
TOTALS			28	154	5317	641	1432	244	49	118	605	485	747	65	.269	.400
Stan Musial 1B90, OF3		L	38	115	341	37	87	13	2	14	44	60	25	0	.255	.428
Don Blasingame 2B150		L	27	150	615	90	178	26	7	1	24	67	42	15	.289	.359
Alex Grammas SS130		R	33	131	368	43	99	14	2	3	30	38	26	3	.269	.342
Ken Boyer 3B143, SS12		R	28	149	563	86	174	18	5	28	94	67	77	12	.309	.508
Joe Cunningham OF121, 1B35		L	27	144	458	65	158	28	6	7	60	88	47	2	.345	.478
Gino Cimoli OF141		R	29	143	519	61	145	40	7	8	72	37	83	7	.279	.430
Bill White OF92, 1B71		L	25	138	517	77	156	33	9	12	72	34	61	15	.302	.470
Hal Smith C141		R	28	142	452	35	122	15	3	13	50	15	28	2	.270	.403
Curt Flood OF106, 2B1		R	21	121	208	24	53	7	3	7	26	16	35	2	.255	.418
George Crowe 1B14		L	36	77	103	14	31	6	0	8	29	5	12	0	.301	.592
Gene Oliver OF42, C9, 1B5		R	23	68	172	14	42	9	0	6	28	7	41	3	.244	.401
1 Ray Jablonski 3B19, SS1		L	32	60	87	11	22	4	0	3	14	8	19	1	.253	.402
Wally Shannon SS21, 2B10		L	25	47	95	5	27	5	0	0	5	0	12	0	.284	.337
Bobby Gene Smith OF32		R	25	43	60	11	13	1	1	1	7	1	9	0	.217	.317
Lee Tate SS39, 2B2, 3B2		R	27	41	50	5	7	1	1	1	4	5	7	0	.140	.260
2 Dick Gray SS13, 3B6, 2B2, OF1		R	27	36	51	9	16	1	0	1	6	6	8	3	.314	.392
Gene Green OF19, C11		R	26	30	74	8	14	6	0	1	3	5	18	0	.189	.311
Solly Hemus 2B1, 3B1		L	36	24	17	2	4	2	0	0	1	8	2	0	.235	.353
2 Jay Porter C19, 1B1		R	26	23	33	5	7	3	0	1	2	1	4	0	.212	.394
1 Chuck Essegian OF9		R	27	17	39	2	7	2	1	0	5	1	13	0	.179	.282
Ray Katt C14		R	31	15	24	0	7	2	0	0	2	0	8	0	.292	.375

Duke Carmel 22 L 3-23, Tim McCarver 17-24, 1 Irv Noren 34 L 1-8, Joe Durham 27 R 0-5, 2 Charlie King 26 R 3-7, Charlie O'Rourke 22 R 0-2

NAME	T	AGE	W	L	PCT	SV	G	GS	CG	IP	H	BB	SO	ShO	ERA
		26	71	83	.461	21	154	154	36	1363	1427	564	846	8	4.34
Lindy McDaniel	R	23	14	12	.538	15	62	7	1	132	144	41	86	0	3.82
Larry Jackson	R	28	14	13	.519	0	40	37	12	256	271	64	145	3	3.30
Vinegar Bend Mizell	L	28	13	10	.565	0	31	30	8	201	196	89	108	1	4.21
Ernie Broglio	R	23	7	12	.368	0	35	25	6	181	174	89	133	3	4.72
Marshall Bridges	L	28	6	3	.667	1	27	4	1	76	67	37	76	0	4.26
Bob Miller	R	20	4	3	.571	0	11	10	3	71	66	21	43	0	3.30
1 Gary Blaylock	R	27	4	5	.444	0	26	12	3	100	117	43	61	0	5.13
Bob Gibson	R	23	3	5	.375	0	13	9	2	76	77	39	48	1	3.32
Alex Kellner (EJ)	L	34	2	1	.667	0	12	4	0	37	31	10	19	0	3.16
Howie Nunn	R	23	2	2	.500	0	16	0	0	21	23	15	20	0	7.71
1 Jim Brosnan	R	29	1	3	.250	2	20	1	0	33	34	15	18	0	4.91
Dick Ricketts	R	25	1	6	.143	0	12	8	0	56	68	30	25	0	5.79
Dean Stone	L	23	0	1	.000	1	18	1	0	30	30	16	17	0	4.20
2 Hal Jeffcoat	R	34	0	1	.000	0	11	0	0	18	33	9	7	0	9.00
Tom Cheney	R	24	0	1	.000	0	11	2	0	12	17	11	8	0	6.75
Bob Duliba	R	24	0	1	.000	1	11	0	0	23	19	12	14	0	2.74
Phil Clark	R	26	0	1	.000	0	7	0	0	7	8	8	5	0	12.86
Bob Blaylock	R	24	0	1	.000	0	3	1	0	9	8	3	3	0	4.00
Tom Hughes	R	24	0	2	.000	0	2	2	0	4	9	2	2	0	15.75
Jack Urban	R	30	0	0	.000	0	8	0	0	11	18	7	4	0	9.00
Bill Smith	L	25	0	0	.000	1	6	0	0	8	11	3	4	0	1.13
Marv Grissom	R	41	0	0	.000	0	3	0	0	2	6	0	0	0	22.50

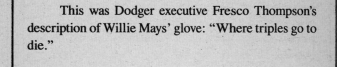

This was Dodger executive Fresco Thompson's description of Willie Mays' glove: "Where triples go to die."

Philadelphia Phillies

There was a strong gravitational pull in Philadelphia in 1959, and for the second year in a row it sucked the Phillies into last place. The club checked into the cellar on May 16 and remained there for all but three days during the remainder of the season.

The only starter with a winning record was 6'8" right-hander Gene Conley, who was dividing his time between the major leagues and professional basketball. Conley in fact did not report to the Phillies until two weeks into the season, having been otherwise occupied helping the Boston Celtics win the NBA championship. The big man put up a 12-7 record until a fractured right hand on August 19 ended his season.

Robin Roberts, on the downhill side of a Hall of Fame career, was 15-17, while Jim Owens at 12-12 was the only other double-figure winner. One-time southpaw ace Curt Simmons was lost for virtually the entire season because of bone chips in his left elbow.

What little punch the club had was supplied by third baseman Gene Freese, who hit 23 home runs, and outfielder Wally Post, who poled 22 long ones. Two-time batting champion Richie Ashburn was at .266, while first-baseman Ed Bouchee led the club with a .285 mark.

Playing his one and only big league season at second base for the Phillies that year (batting just .218) was 25-year-old George (Sparky) Anderson.

"He always had a keen, analytical mind," Sawyer said. "I wasn't at all surprised when he went on to become a successful manager."

Robin Roberts. One of the great pitchers in baseball history, the Phillies' right-hander was beginning the downhill slide in 1959.

Two-time National League batting champion Richie Ashburn.   *L.*

This 25-year-old gentleman played his only big-league season in 1959. His .218 batting average suggested that his future lay elsewhere. It did, but not too far away. You're looking at George Lee (Sparky) Anderson.   *R.*

For Sawyer, who had won a pennant managing the Phillies in 1950, managing the club had been a draining experience. The following spring, seeing that things weren't going to get any better, he resigned after opening day. Why?

"I was forty-nine years old," Eddie said, "and I wanted to live to be fifty."

⚾

NAME	G by POS	B	AGE	G	AB	R	H	2B	3B	HR	RBI	BB	SO	SB	BA	SA
PHILADELPHIA 8th 64-90 .416 23							EDDIE SAWYER									
TOTALS			30	155	5109	599	1237	196	38	113	560	498	858	39	.242	.362
Ed Bouchee	1B134	L	26	136	499	75	142	29	4	15	74	70	74	0	.285	.449
Sparky Anderson																
	2B152	R	25	152	477	42	104	9	3	0	34	42	53	6	.218	.249
Joe Koppe	SS113, 2B11	R	28	126	422	68	110	18	7	7	28	41	80	7	.261	.386
Gene Freese	3B109,															
	2B6	R	25	132	400	60	107	14	5	23	70	43	61	8	.268	.500
Wally Post	OF120	L	29	132	468	62	119	17	6	22	94	36	101	0	.254	.457
Richie Ashburn	OF149	L	32	153	564	86	150	16	2	1	20	79	42	9	.266	.307
Harry Anderson	OF137	L	27	142	508	50	122	28	6	14	63	43	95	1	.240	.402
Carl Sawatski	C89	L	31	74	198	15	58	10	0	9	43	32	36	0	.293	.480
Dave Philley	OF34,															
	1B24	B	39	99	254	32	74	18	2	7	37	18	27	0	.291	.461
2 Solly Drake	OF37	B	28	67	62	10	9	1	0	0	3	8	15	5	.145	.161
Valmy Thomas	C63,															
	3B1	R	30	66	140	5	28	2	0	1	7	9	19	1	.200	.236
Harry Hanebrink	2B15,															
	3B9, OF1	L	31	57	97	10	25	3	1	1	7	2	12	0	.258	.340
Bob Bowman	OF20, P5	R	28	57	79	7	10	0	0	2	5	5	23	0	.127	.203
1 Willie Jones	3B46	R	33	47	160	23	43	9	1	7	24	19	14	0	.269	.469
Chico Fernandez	SS40,															
	2B2	R	27	45	123	15	26	5	1	0	3	10	11	2	.211	.268
Joe Lonnett	C43	R	32	43	93	8	16	1	0	1	10	14	17	0	.172	.215
1 Jim Hegan	C25	R	38	25	51	1	10	1	0	0	8	3	10	0	.196	.216
1 Granny Hamner																
	SS15, 3B1	R	32	21	64	10	19	4	0	2	6	5	5	0	.297	.453
2 Jim Bolger 27 R 4-48, John Easton 26 R 0-3																

NAME	T	AGE	W	L	PCT	SV	G	GS	CG	IP	H	BB	SO	ShO	ERA
		29	64	90	.416	15	155	155	54	1354	1357	474	769	8	4.27
Robin Roberts	R	32	15	17	.469	0	35	35	19	257	267	35	137	2	4.27
Gene Conley (BH)	R	28	12	7	.632	1	25	22	12	180	159	42	102	3	3.00
Jim Owens	R	25	12	12	.500	1	31	30	11	221	203	73	135	1	3.22
Don Cardwell	R	23	9	10	.474	0	25	22	5	153	135	65	106	1	4.06
Jack Meyer	R	27	5	3	.625	1	47	1	1	94	76	53	71	0	3.35
Ruben Gomez	R	31	3	8	.273	1	20	12	2	72	90	24	37	1	6.13
Ray Semproch	R	28	3	10	.231	3	30	18	2	112	119	59	54	0	5.38
2 Humberto Robinson	R	29	2	4	.333	1	31	4	1	73	70	24	32	0	3.33
1 Al Schroll	R	27	1	1	.500	0	3	0	0	9	12	6	4	0	9.00
2 Taylor Phillips	L	26	1	4	.200	1	32	3	1	63	72	31	35	0	5.00
Dick Farrell	R	25	1	6	.143	6	38	0	0	57	61	25	31	0	4.74
Bob Bowman	R	28	0	1	.000	0	5	0	0	6	5	5	0	0	6.00
Jim Hearn	R	38	0	2	.000	0	6	0	0	11	15	6	1	0	5.73
1 Seth Morehead	L	24	0	2	.000	0	3	3	0	10	15	3	8	0	9.90
Ed Keegan	R	19	0	3	.000	0	3	3	0	9	19	13	3	0	18.00
Curt Simmons (SA)	L	30	0	0	.000	0	7	0	0	10	16	0	4	0	4.50
Chris Short	L	21	0	0	.000	0	3	2	0	14	19	10	8	0	8.38
Freddy Rodriguez	R	31	0	0	.000	0	1	0	0	2	4	0	1	0	13.50

The American League Pennant Race

　　　　At first glance, the American League pennant race in 1959 looked like a case of startling contrasts. The winners were the Chicago White Sox, who had not won a pennant in 40 years, not since their professional ancestors of 1919, who had won it and then disgraced themselves by throwing the World Series. Almost as surprising as the team who won it was the team who did not—Casey Stengel's New York Yankees, who had given a rubber-stamp quality to American League races by winning nine of the last ten years.

　　　　At second glance, however, it was not quite as startling as it seemed. The White Sox had finished third five years in a row, and then, under Al Lopez, second in 1957 and 1958. If ever a team has been priming itself in long rehearsal, it was the White Sox.

　　　　Indications that this was not going to be a Yankee year came early. On May 11, Stengel's team dropped into last place and remained there for 11 days. They had a resurgent June, climbed to within $1\frac{1}{2}$ games at the end of the month, but thereafter fell back and ceased to be a factor, particularly after losing five straight at Fenway Park from July 9–13.

　　　　After the All-Star break, the race settled down to a grueling battle between the White Sox and Joe Gordon's Cleveland Indians. Neither club played under .500 in any month all summer long. The Indians got off to a running start by winning ten of their first 11 and led most of the time until mid-July, with their biggest advantage being $3\frac{1}{2}$ games. But the White Sox kept coming, playing sizzling ball in midsummer—20-7 in July and then 21-9 in August. During a red-hot home stand at the end of July, during which they won 11 of 12, the White Sox moved into first place on July 28 and were never out of it again.

By the middle of August, the White Sox had drawn in front by $4\frac{1}{2}$ games, with a strong pitching staff working like so many well-oiled machines. But then the Indians suddenly surged again, winning eight in a row from August 19–26 and drawing to within one game of the Sox.

The two contenders then squared off for a critical four-game series at Cleveland on August 28–30. In its timing, it was a schedule maker's delight; it was also a delight for Cleveland's financial ledgers, as over 70,000 fans turned out for the Friday night game and over 66,000 for the Sunday doubleheader. Artistically, however, it was a lost weekend for the Indians, as Lopez's team swept all four games—7-3 behind Bob Shaw, a 2-0 shutout by Dick Donovan, and then 6-3 and 9-4 behind Early Wynn and Barry Latman.

It was on their next visit to Cleveland, on September 22, that the White Sox clinched the pennant, Wynn defeating the Indians, 4-3. With a 94-60 record, Chicago's final margin over the Indians was five games. The White Sox won when it mattered—they were 15-7 for the year with Cleveland, and therein lay the difference.

"All we had to do was play them .500," said Indians skipper Joe Gordon, "and we would have won it."

The American League Teams That Year

Chicago White Sox

They called the 1959 White Sox "The Go-Go Sox" because of the club's aggressive running game. The White Sox' 113 stolen bases may seem small potatoes by later standards, but this was the highest total in the league since 1945. The primary base thief was shortstop Luis Aparicio with 56—almost half the club's total and more than the totals of six other American League teams. Aparicio was in the midst of leading the league in stolen bases nine years in a row—his first nine years in the majors. (His winged feet and sensational defensive work would eventually land him in the Hall of Fame.)

Aparicio's infield partner, second baseman Nellie Fox, was the league's Most Valuable Player (Luis was runner-up). Fox won the designation on the strength of his .306 batting average, perpetual hustle, and sharp fielding—he and Aparicio each led in fielding percentage at their respective positions. Uncanny at bat, Fox fanned just 13 times in 624 official appearances. Paul Richards, who had managed Fox a few years earlier, called Nellie "the most spirited and aggressive player" he had ever seen.

At first base, Lopez rotated former National Leaguer Earl Torgeson, rookie Norm Cash, and another former National Leaguer, Ted Kluszewski, picked up from Pittsburgh on August 25. (The Sox made a mistake by trading Cash to Cleveland in December, and Cleveland repeated the mistake by trading him to Detroit in April 1960. Norm then went on to a long, home-run-hitting career for the Tigers.)

Bubba Phillips and former Red Sox batting champion Billy Goodman shared third base, as Lopez juggled and

Luis Aparicio, whose magic glove earned him a place in the Hall of Fame. L.

Nelson Fox, American League MVP in 1959 and one of baseball's great non-stop hustlers. R.

maneuvered his light-hitting lineup all summer. Defensive whiz Jim Landis held down center field, flanked at one time or another by Jim McAnany, Al Smith, Jim Rivera and young Johnny Callison. (The Sox made another trading blunder that December when they sent the talented 20-year-old Callison to the Phillies in exchange for third-baseman Gene Freese.)

The bulk of the catching was done by Sherman Lollar, who also did most of the club's power hitting, leading his mates with 22 home runs and 84 runs batted in. Lollar was also something of a blithe spirit. Once, during a pre-game chat with opposing catcher Clint Courtney on a blazing hot day, Sherm threw his arm affectionately around Courtney's

Al Lopez, a big-league manager for 17 years. He won two pennants and finished second ten times. Al's pennants with Cleveland in 1954 and Chicago in 1959 were the only ones the Yankees didn't win from 1949-1964. L.

White Sox catcher Sherman Lollar. R.

shoulders and, while chatting, rubbed limburger cheese all over the back of Clint's uniform blouse. By the second inning, the odor rising from Courtney was overpowering and the home plate umpire, who was getting the full benefit of it, ordered him to the clubhouse to change. It was a practical joke with lingering effects.

"We did it on speed, defense, and pitching," Lopez said. "We had a gung-ho, one-for-all, all-for-one kind of club and they really put it together."

A glance at the records supports the skipper. Although Chicago's .250 team batting average was bettered by five other teams, their 97 home runs were the fewest in the league, and five other teams outscored them, they led in fielding and stolen bases. On top of that, their pitching staff logged the lowest earned-run average in the league—3.29.

Early Wynn was the ace. The former Cleveland Indian right-hander was 22-10 (the league's only 20-game winner). At the age of 39, Wynn started 37 games, the most in the league that year. He was particularly effective against his old team, beating the Indians in six of seven contests.

Another right-hander, Bob Shaw, was 18-6, his .750 winning percentage the league's best. Bob's favorite teams were Kansas City and Washington—he was 9-0 against them. The club's long-time ace, southpaw Billy Pierce, was 14-15.

Lopez had the benefit this year of some superb relief pitching from a pair of National League veterans, right-handers Turk Lown and Gerry Staley. Appearing in 60 games, Lown was 9-2, with 15 saves; and Staley, in a league-high 67 games, was 8-5, with 14 saves. Another starter, Dick Donovan, who Ted Williams said threw the toughest slider he ever batted against, was 9-10.

Underlining the character of their play that year, the White Sox were 35-15 in one-run games, three under the league record of 38 set by the Yankees in 1943.

Casey Stengel was always in awe of the physical strength of his star, Mickey Mantle. One day, after Mickey had been dusted off a few times by Washington pitchers, Casey said, "They've gotta have rocks in their heads to throw at him. And if he ever decides to come out there after them, they'd better have rocks in their hands."

NAME	G by POS	B	AGE	G	AB	R	H	2B	3B	HR	RBI	BB	SO	SB	BA	SA
CHICAGO 1st 94-60 .610							AL LOPEZ									
TOTALS			30	156	5297	669	1325	220	46	97	620	580	634	113	.250	.364
Earl Torgeson	1B103	L	35	127	277	40	61	5	3	9	45	62	55	7	.220	.357
Nellie Fox	2B156	L	31	156	624	84	191	34	6	2	70	71	13	5	.306	.389
Luis Aparicio	SS152	R	25	152	612	98	157	18	5	6	51	52	40	56	.257	.332
Bubba Phillips	3B100, OF23	R	29	117	379	43	100	27	1	5	40	27	28	1	.264	.380
Jim McAnany	OF67	R	22	67	210	22	58	9	3	0	27	19	26	2	.276	.348
Jim Landis	OF148	R	25	149	515	78	140	26	7	5	60	78	68	20	.272	.379
Al Smith	OF128, 3B1	R	31	129	472	65	112	16	4	17	55	46	74	7	.237	.396
Sherm Lollar	C122, 1B24	R	34	140	505	63	134	22	3	22	84	55	49	4	.265	.451
Billy Goodman	3B74, 2B3	L	33	104	268	21	67	14	1	1	28	19	20	3	.250	.321
Jim Rivera	OF69	L	36	80	177	18	3	9	4	4	19	11	19	5	.220	.384
Sammy Esposito	3B45, SS14, 2B2	R	27	69	66	12	11	1	0	1	5	11	16	0	.167	.227
Norm Cash	1B31	L	24	58	104	16	25	0	1	4	16	18	9	1	.240	.375
Johnny Romano	C38	R	24	53	126	20	37	5	1	5	25	23	18	0	.294	.458
Johnny Callison	OF41	L	20	49	104	12	18	3	0	3	12	13	20	0	.173	.288
2 Harry Simpson	OF12, 1B1	L	33	38	75	5	14	5	1	2	13	4	14	0	.187	.360
2 Ted Kluszewski	1B29	L	34	31	101	11	30	2	1	2	10	9	10	0	.297	.396
2 Del Ennis	OF25	R	34	26	96	10	21	6	0	2	7	4	10	0	.219	.344
Earl Battey	C20	R	24	26	64	9	14	1	2	2	7	8	13	0	.219	.391
2 Larry Doby (BN)	OF12, 1B2	L	35	21	58	1	14	1	1	0	9	2	13	1	.241	.293
Ron Jackson	1B5	R	25	10	14	3	3	1	0	1	2	1	0	0	.214	.500

1 Ray Boone 35 R 5-21, Lou Skizas 27 R 1-13, Joe Hicks 26 L 3-7, Don Mueller 32 L 2-4, J. C. Martin 22 L 1-4, Cam Carreon 21 R 0-1

NAME	T	AGE	W	L	PCT	SV	G	GS	CG	IP	H	BB	SO	ShO	ERA
		32	94	60	.610	36	156	156	44	1425	1297	525	761	13	3.29
Early Wynn	R	39	22	10	.688	0	37	37	14	256	202	119	179	5	3.16
Bob Shaw	R	26	18	6	.750	3	47	26	8	231	217	54	89	3	2.69
Billy Pierce	L	32	14	15	.483	0	34	33	12	224	217	62	114	2	3.62
Turk Lown	R	35	9	2	.818	15	60	0	0	93	73	42	63	0	2.90
Dick Donovan	R	31	9	10	.474	0	31	29	5	180	171	58	71	1	3.65
Gerry Staley	R	38	8	5	.615	14	67	0	0	116	111	25	54	0	2.25
Barry Latman	R	23	8	5	.615	0	37	21	5	156	138	72	97	2	3.75
Ray Moore	R	33	3	6	.333	0	29	8	0	90	86	46	49	0	4.10
Rudy Arias	L	28	2	0	1.000	2	34	0	0	44	49	20	28	0	4.09
Joe Stanka	R	27	1	0	1.000	0	2	0	0	5	2	4	3	0	3.60
Ken McBride	R	23	0	1	.000	1	11	2	0	23	20	17	12	0	3.13
1 Don Rudolph	L	27	0	0	.000	0	4	0	0	3	4	2	0	0	0.00
Claude Raymond	R	22	0	0	.000	0	3	0	0	4	5	2	1	0	9.00
Gary Peters	L	22	0	0	.000	0	2	0	0	1	2	2	1	0	0.00

Cleveland Indians

The strongest-hitting team in the American League in 1959 was second-place Cleveland. Joe Gordon's team led in batting (.263), slugging (.408), runs scored (745), and home runs (167). They also had the home-run leader in Rocky Colavito, who hit 42 (tied by Harmon Killebrew). Rocky's 111 runs batted in were one behind the league leader, Boston's Jackie Jensen. Abetting Rocky in the long-ball department were infielder Woodie Held (29 home runs), outfielder Minnie Miñoso (21), and outfielder/first baseman Tito Francona (20). Francona had a sensational year, batting .363, but his 399 official at-bats fell short of qualifying him for the batting title. At .302, Miñoso was the team's leading hitter, followed by flashy-fielding first-baseman Vic Power, at .289.

The Indians lacked a regular third baseman that year. Held and George Strickland shared the bag with numerous others during the course of the season; and these same two players also split the shortstop position between them. (Held, who could also give you a game in the outfield, possessed one of the strongest throwing arms in the league.)

It is interesting to note that the Indians' roster included two of the most volatile characters in the league that year. At one time, Billy Martin (then a Yankee) and Jimmy Piersall (then a Red Sox) had engaged in a notorious fistfight. Now they were teammates: Jimmy in center field and Billy at second base. Billy's year was twice interrupted, once for three weeks in June and July by a shoulder injury, and then for the rest of the season, after he was hit in the face on August 5th by a pitched ball delivered by Washington's Truman

Cleveland first-baseman Vic Power. A flashy fielder, he was taking throws and catching pop flies with one hand before the style became fashionable.

Clevenger. Billy suffered fractures of the jaw and cheekbone. (Billy's troubles didn't begin with George Steinbrenner.)

Future big-league skipper Russ Nixon shared the catch-

Right-hander Jim Grant, nicknamed "Mudcat."

ing with Ed Fitzgerald and Dick Brown, none of the three causing much fuss at home plate.

Right-hander Cal McLish led the pitchers with a 19-8 record. Cal, whose full name was Calvin Coolidge Julius Caesar Tuskahoma McLish (he was known as "Buster" to his teammates), was particularly effective against rugged opposition, being 4-1 versus the White Sox and 6-1 over the Yankees.

Gary Bell was 16-11, Jim Perry 12-10, and Mudcat Grant 10-7, while left-hander Herb Score was 9-11. Score was 7-3 in mid-June and seemed on the way back after missing most of the previous two years with injuries, but he failed to win a single game after July 3.

NAME	G by POS	B	AGE	G	AB	R	H	2B	3B	HR	RBI	BB	SO	SB	BA	SA
CLEVELAND 2nd 89-65 .578 5								JOE GORDON								
TOTALS			29	154	5288	745	1390	216	25	167	682	433	721	33	.263	.408
Vic Power 1B121, 2B21,																
	3B7	R	27	145	595	102	172	31	6	10	60	40	22	9	.289	.412
Billy Martin (SJ-BY)																
	2B67, 3B4	R	31	73	242	37	63	7	0	9	24	7	18	0	.260	.401
Woodie Held SS103,																
	3B40, OF6, 2B3	R	27	143	525	82	132	19	3	29	71	47	118	1	.251	.465
George Strickland																
	3B80, SS50, 2B4	R	33	132	441	55	105	15	2	3	48	52	64	1	.238	.302
Rocky Colavito OF154		R	25	154	588	90	151	24	0	42	111	71	86	3	.257	.512
Jimmy Piersall OF91,																
	3B1	R	29	100	317	42	78	13	2	4	30	24	31	6	.246	.338
Minnie Miñoso OF148		R	36	148	570	92	172	32	0	21	92	54	46	8	.302	.468
Russ Nixon C74		L	24	82	258	23	62	10	3	1	29	15	28	0	.240	.314
Tito Francona OF64,																
	1B35	L	25	122	399	68	145	17	2	20	79	35	42	2	.363	.566
2 Jim Baxes 2B48,																
	3B22	R	30	77	247	35	59	11	0	15	34	21	47	0	.239	.466
2 Ed Fitz Gerald (BG)																
	C45	R	35	49	129	12	35	6	1	1	4	12	14	0	.271	.357
Dick Brown C48		R	24	48	141	15	31	7	0	5	16	11	39	0	.220	.376
Ray Webster 2B24,																
	3B4	R	21	40	74	10	15	2	1	2	10	5	7	1	.203	.338
Elmer Valo OF2		L	38	34	24	3	7	0	0	0	5	7	0	0	.292	.292
Carroll Hardy OF15		R	26	32	53	12	11	1	0	0	2	3	7	1	.208	.226
2 Granny Hamner																
	SS10, 2B7, 3B5	R	32	27	67	4	11	1	1	1	3	1	8	0	.164	.254
1 Hal Naragon C10		L	30	14	36	6	10	4	1	0	5	3	2	0	.278	.444
Chuck Tanner OF10		L	29	14	48	6	12	2	0	1	5	2	9	0	.250	.354
Gene Leek 3B13, SS1		R	22	13	36	7	8	3	0	1	5	2	7	0	.222	.389
2 Willie Jones 33 R 4-18, Don Dillard 22 L 4-10, Billy Moran 25 R 5-17, 1Jim Bolger 27 R 0-7, Gordy Coleman 24 L 8-15, 1 Randy Jackson 33 R 1-7																

NAME	T	AGE	W	L	PCT	SV	G	GS	CG	IP	H	BB	SO	ShO	ERA
		27	89	65	.578	23	154	154	58	1384	1230	635	799	7	3.75
Cal McLish	R	33	19	8	.704	1	35	32	13	235	253	72	113	0	3.64
Gary Bell	R	22	16	11	.593	5	44	28	12	234	208	105	136	1	4.04
Jim Perry	R	23	12	10	.545	4	44	13	8	153	122	55	79	2	2.65
Mudcat Grant	R	23	10	7	.588	3	38	19	6	165	140	81	85	1	4.15
Herb Score	L	26	9	11	.450	0	30	25	9	161	123	115	147	1	4.70
3 Jack Harshman	L	31	5	1	.833	1	13	6	5	66	46	13	35	1	2.59
Don Ferrarese	L	30	5	3	.625	0	15	10	4	76	58	51	45	0	3.20
Al Cicotte	R	29	3	1	.750	1	26	1	0	44	46	25	23	0	5.32
Bobby Locke	R	25	3	2	.600	2	24	7	0	78	66	41	40	0	3.12
Mike Garcia	R	25	3	6	.333	1	29	8	1	72	72	31	49	0	4.00
Dick Brodowski	R	26	2	2	.500	5	18	0	0	30	19	21	9	0	1.80
1 Humberto Robinson	R	29	1	0	1.000	0	5	0	0	9	9	4	6	0	4.00
Jake Striker	L	25	1	0	1.000	0	1	1	0	7	8	4	5	0	2.57
2 Riverboat Smith	L	31	0	1	.000	0	12	3	0	29	31	12	17	0	5.28
Bud Podbielan	R	35	0	0	.000	0	6	0	0	12	17	2	5	0	6.00
Johnny Briggs	R	25	0	1	.000	0	4	1	0	13	12	3	5	0	2.08

A well-known American League pitcher was telling some teammates about the misfortune that had befallen him one night when he was pitching in Triple-A.

"It was the eighth inning of a tie ball game," the pitcher said, "the bases were loaded and there were two out. I throw my best curve ball and the guy hits it on two easy hops to the shortstop. Your grandmother could have made this play. But what do you think the SOB does? He takes the ball and heaves it ten feet over the first baseman's head and all three runs score. That's the kind of support I had in Triple-A."

"I want to ask you one question," one of the pitcher's teammates said.

"What's that?" the pitcher asked.

"How did the bases get loaded?"

"Mind your damned business," the pitcher said.

New York Yankees

The Yankees had finished poorly in 1958, playing under .500 ball the last two months. And they began poorly in 1959, going 19-23 for April and May. Casey Stengel's team played well in June (18-12), but sank in July (12-16) and never resurfaced as a threat. It was only the second time in 11 years that Stengel's team had failed to win. (The Yankees would atone by winning the next five pennants in a row.)

In baseball, we don't always know *why* something happened, but we do always know *what* happened, and in 1959 it was fairly clear what happened to the Yankees. In 1958, Mickey Mantle hit 42 home runs and batted .304; in 1959, he hit only 31 homers and batted .285. In 1958, Elston Howard batted .314; in 1959, it was .272. In 1958, Norm Siebern batted .300; in 1959 he batted .271. Most devastating of all, in 1958, Bob Turley was 21-7; in 1959, he was 8-11. In addition, first baseman Bill Skowron, batting a highly productive .298 at the time, suffered a fractured wrist on July 25 and was lost for the remainder of the season. Replacing him was that future symbol of New York Mets ineptitude, Marv Throneberry. Then a highly regarded young power hitter, Marv got into 80 games, batted .240, hit eight home runs, and was soon no longer highly regarded.

Turning in a fine year for the Yankees was their 23-year-old second baseman, Bobby Richardson, who led the team with a .301 average. With shortstop Tony Kubek, he was part of one of the snappiest double-play combinations in the league. Third base was shared by Hector Lopez, who simply couldn't play it (a .926 fielding average for 76 games), and

Mickey Mantle.   *L.*

Bobby Richardson, the only Yankee to bat over .300 in 1959. R.

those two models of versatility, Kubek and Gil McDougald, plus Andy Carey. Behind the plate was Yogi Berra, 34 years old now, but still catching 116 games and batting .284.

Whitey Ford led the staff with a 16-10 record, followed by Duke Maas at 14-8 and Art Ditmar at 13-9. Ryne Duren, a near-sighted fireballer, was spectacular in relief. Although his won-lost record was just 3-6, he saved 14 games, fanned 96 in 77 innings, and had a 1.87 ERA. On June 1, big Don Larsen was 6-1, but never won another game for the rest of the year, finishing with a 6-7 record.

The Yankees continued picking away at the Kansas City roster. On May 26, they dispatched pitchers Johnny Kucks and Tom Sturdivant and infielder Jerry Lumpe to KC in

Yogi Berra.

exchange for Lopez and pitcher Ralph Terry, whom they had traded to the KC club two years before. Although the Yankees finished a distant third in 1959, they bounced back in a big way and won the next five American League pennants (1960-1964).

Whitey Ford, greatest of all Yankee pitchers.

NAME	G by POS	B	AGE	G	AB	R	H	2B	3B	HR	RBI	BB	SO	SB	BA	SA
NEW YORK 3rd 79-75 .513 15							CASEY STENGEL									
TOTALS			28	115	5379	687	1397	224	40	153	651	457	828	45	.260	.402
Bill Skowron (XJ) 1B72		R	28	74	282	39	84	13	5	15	59	20	47	1	.298	.539
Bobby Richardson 2B109, SS14, 3B12		R	23	134	469	53	141	18	6	2	33	26	20	5	.301	.377
Tony Kubek SS67, OF53, 3B17, 2B1		L	22	132	512	67	143	25	7	6	51	24	46	3	.279	.391
2 Hector Lopez 3B76, OF35		R	26	112	406	60	115	16	2	16	69	28	54	3	.283	.451
Hank Bauer OF111		R	36	114	341	44	81	20	0	9	39	33	54	4	.238	.375
Mickey Mantle OF143		B	27	144	541	104	154	23	4	31	75	93	126	21	.285	.514
Norm Siebern OF93, 1B2		L	25	120	380	52	103	17	0	11	53	41	71	3	.271	.403
Yogi Berra C116, OF7		L	34	131	472	64	134	25	1	19	69	43	38	1	.284	.462
Gil McDougald 2B53, SS52, 3B25		R	31	127	434	44	109	16	8	4	34	35	40	0	.251	.353
Elston Howard 1B50, C43, OF28		R	30	125	443	59	121	24	6	18	73	20	57	0	.273	.476
Marv Throneberry 1B54, OF13		L	25	80	192	27	46	5	0	8	22	18	51	0	.240	.391
1 Enos Slaughter OF26		L	43	74	99	10	17	2	0	6	21	13	19	1	.172	.374
Johnny Blanchard C12, OF8, 1B1		L	26	49	59	6	10	1	0	2	4	7	12	0	.169	.288
Clete Boyer SS26, 3B16		R	22	47	114	4	20	2	0	0	3	6	23	1	.175	.193
Andy Carey (IL) 3B34		R	27	41	101	11	26	1	0	3	9	7	17	1	.257	.356
Fritzie Brickell SS15, 2B3		R	24	18	39	4	10	1	0	1	4	1	10	0	.256	.359
1 Jerry Lumpe 3B12, SS4, 2B1		L	26	18	45	2	10	0	0	0	2	6	7	0	.222	.222
2 Jim Pisoni OF15		R	29	17	17	2	3	1	0	1	1	1	9	0	.176	.294

Gordon Windhorn 25 R 0-11, Ken Hunt 24 R 4-12

NAME	T	AGE	W	L	PCT	SV	G	GS	CG	IP	H	BB	SO	ShO	ERA
		28	79	75	.513	28	155	155	38	1399	1281	594	836	15	3.60
Whitey Ford	L	30	16	10	.615	1	35	29	9	204	194	89	114	2	3.04
Duke Maas	R	30	14	8	.636	4	38	21	3	138	149	53	67	1	4.43
Art Ditmar	R	30	13	9	.591	7	38	25	7	202	156	52	96	1	2.90
Bob Turley	R	28	8	11	.421	0	33	22	7	154	141	83	111	3	4.32
Bobby Shantz	L	33	7	3	.700	3	33	4	2	95	64	33	66	2	2.37
Jim Coates	R	26	6	1	.857	3	37	4	2	100	89	36	64	0	2.88
Don Larsen	R	29	6	7	.462	0	25	18	3	125	122	76	69	1	4.32
Ryne Duren	R	30	3	6	.333	14	41	0	0	77	49	43	96	0	1.87
2 Ralph Terry	R	23	3	7	.300	0	24	16	5	127	130	30	55	1	3.40
Eli Grba	R	24	2	5	.286	0	19	6	0	50	52	39	23	0	6.48
John Gabler	R	28	1	1	.500	0	3	1	0	19	21	10	11	0	2.84
2 Gary Blaylock	R	27	0	1	.000	0	15	1	0	26	30	15	20	0	3.46
1 Johnny Kucks	R	25	0	1	.000	0	9	1	0	17	21	9	9	0	8.47
1 Tom Sturdivant	R	29	0	2	.000	0	7	3	0	25	20	9	16	0	5.04
Jim Bronstad	R	23	0	3	.000	2	16	3	0	29	34	13	14	0	5.28
Zack Monroe	R	27	0	0	.000	0	3	0	0	3	3	2	1	0	6.00
1 Mark Freeman	R	28	0	0	.000	0	1	1	0	7	6	2	4	0	2.57

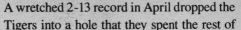

Detroit Tigers

A wretched 2-13 record in April dropped the Tigers into a hole that they spent the rest of the season trying to climb out of. After the club had lost 15 of its first 17, they also lost their manager, Bill Norman, who had taken over the previous June. Norman was replaced by Jimmy Dykes, who had been coaching for the Pittsburgh Pirates. Jimmy proved a tonic, and the Tigers immediately went on a rampage, winning 32 of their next 46 and climbing to within a half-game of first place on June 20. That, however, proved to be high tide for Detroit. A 12-18 July all but finished them off.

Even so, the Tigers received top-drawer individual performances from their "K-Men," Harvey Kuenn and Al Kaline. Kuenn, who had been converted from shortstop to the outfield the year before, line-drived his way to the batting title with a .353 average, leading also with 198 hits (the fourth time he had topped the league in hits) and 42 doubles.

Kaline, at the age of 24 in his seventh big league season, batted .327 and hit 27 home runs, while driving in 94 runs, despite missing several weeks with a broken jaw.

Third-baseman Eddie Yost, acquired from Washington the previous December, led the league in walks (for the fifth time), with 135 and runs with 115; he also hit 21 homers and batted .278. Second-baseman Frank Bolling batted .266 and excelled in the field, making just eight errors in 126 games. (Detroit's 124 errors were the fewest in the league.) Former National Leaguer Rocky Bridges batted .268. First base, however, was Detroit's weak link that year; the bag was shared by Gail Harris, who batted .221, and Bobo Osborne, whose average was an anemic .191. The catching was divided

Harvey Kuenn, American League batting champion in 1959. L.

Al Kaline, just 24 years old in 1959. Ahead lay a total of 3,000 hits and a Hall of Fame plaque.   *R.*

between Lou Berberet (.216) and Red Wilson (.263). Outfielder Charlie Maxwell generated some real power with 31 homers and 95 RBIs. Charlie had a knack of hitting home runs on Sunday, when the crowds were largest, thus becoming one of the Tigers' most popular players. In fact, Maxwell hit 21 of his 31 dingers at home. Overall, 200 home runs were hit in Detroit's Briggs Stadium in 1959, far more than in any other American League park.

The Tigers had a trio of 17-game winners at the top of their staff in lefty Don Mossi (17-9), Frank Lary (17-10) and Jim Bunning (17-13). Bunning was the strikeout leader, with 201. Mossi and Lary were particularly effective against the Yankees, Mossi going 6-2 against Stengel's team and Lary,

Jim Bunning, ace pitcher for Detroit and future Republican Congressman from the State of Kentucky.

5-1. For Lary, it was business as usual—he was 28-13 (lifetime) versus the Yankees, at the time baseball's top club.

The Tigers suffered from bullpen weakness in 1959, with neither Ray Narleski (4-12) nor Tom Morgan (1-4) proving very successful in stemming the late-inning tides.

NAME	G by POS	B	AGE	G	AB	R	H	2B	3B	HR	RBI	BB	SO	SB	BA	SA
DETROIT 4th 76-78 .494 18					BILL NORMAN 2-15 .118		JIMMY DYKES 74-63 .540									
TOTALS			28	154	5211	713	1346	196	30	160	667	580	737	34	.258	.400
Gail Harris	1B93	L	27	114	349	39	77	4	3	9	39	29	49	0	.221	.327
Frank Bolling	2B126	R	27	127	459	56	122	18	3	13	55	45	37	2	.266	.403
Rocky Bridges	SS110	R	31	116	381	38	102	16	3	3	35	30	35	1	.268	.349
Eddie Yost	3B146, 2B1	R	32	148	521	115	145	19	0	21	61	135	77	9	.278	.436
Harvey Kuenn	OF137	R	28	139	561	99	198	42	7	9	71	48	37	7	.353	.501
Al Kaline	OF136	R	24	136	511	86	167	19	2	27	94	72	42	10	.327	.530
Charlie Maxwell	OF136	L	32	145	518	81	130	12	2	31	95	81	91	0	.251	.461
Lou Berberet	C95	L	29	100	338	38	73	8	2	13	44	35	59	0	.216	.367
Bobo Osborne	1B56, OF1	L	23	86	209	27	40	7	1	3	21	16	41	1	.191	.278
Coot Veal	SS72	R	26	77	89	12	18	1	0	1	15	8	7	0	.202	.247
2 Ted Lepcio	SS35, 2B24, 3B11	R	28	76	215	25	60	8	0	7	24	17	49	2	.279	.414
Red Wilson	C64	R	30	67	228	28	60	17	2	4	35	10	23	2	.263	.408
Neil Christley	OF21	L	27	65	106	7	14	3	0	6	11	12	10	0	.132	.330
Gus Zernial	1B32, OF1	R	36	60	132	11	30	4	0	7	26	7	27	0	.227	.417
Johnny Groth	OF41	R	32	55	102	12	24	7	1	1	10	7	14	0	.235	.353
1 Larry Doby	OF16	L	35	18	55	5	12	3	1	0	4	8	9	0	.218	.309

Steve Demeter 24 R 2-18, Ossie Alvarez 25 R 1-2, Ron Shoop 27 R 1-7, Charlie Lau 26 L 1-6

NAME	T	AGE	W	L	PCT	SV	G	GS	CG	IP	H	BB	SO	ShO	ERA
		29	76	78	.494	24	154	154	53	1360	1327	432	829	9	4.20
Don Mossi	L	30	17	9	.654	0	34	30	15	228	210	49	125	3	3.36
Frank Lary	R	29	17	10	.630	0	32	32	11	223	225	46	137	3	3.55
Jim Bunning	R	27	17	13	.567	1	40	35	14	250	220	75	201	1	3.89
Paul Foytack	R	28	14	14	.500	1	39	37	11	240	239	64	110	2	4.65
Ray Narleski	R	30	4	12	.250	5	42	10	1	104	105	59	71	0	5.80
Jerry Davie	R	26	2	2	.500	0	11	5	1	37	40	17	20	0	4.14
1 Billy Hoeft	L	27	1	1	.500	0	2	2	0	9	6	4	2	0	5.00
Barney Schultz	R	32	1	2	.333	0	13	0	0	18	17	14	17	0	4.50
2 Dave Sisler	R	27	1	3	.250	7	32	0	0	52	46	36	29	0	3.98
Pete Burnside	L	28	1	3	.250	1	30	0	0	62	55	25	49	0	3.77
Tom Morgan	R	29	1	4	.200	9	46	1	0	93	94	18	39	0	3.97
Bob Bruce	R	26	0	1	.000	0	2	1	0	2	2	3	1	0	9.00
Jim Proctor	R	23	0	1	.000	0	2	1	0	3	8	3	0	0	15.00
2 Bob Smith	L	28	0	3	.000	0	9	0	0	11	20	3	10	0	8.18
George Susce	R	27	0	0	.000	0	9	0	0	15	24	9	9	0	12.60
Jim Stump	R	27	0	0	.000	0	5	0	0	11	12	4	6	0	2.45
Hank Aguirre	L	27	0	0	.000	0	3	0	0	3	4	3	3	0	3.00

Boston Red Sox

The Boston Red Sox dropped from third in 1953 to fifth in 1959. Along the way, they lost their manager Pinky Higgins (after 72 games). Pinky was replaced by former National League shortstop Billy Jurges, under whom the club perked up, playing .550 ball, compared to .425 under Higgins. The only club in the league to play better ball than Boston over the last two months of the season was the pennant-winning White Sox (Boston was 31-22 in August and September, but all it got them was fifth place).

As ever, all eyes in Boston were on Ted Williams, now in his eighteenth season. Unfortunately, they saw the greatest hitter in baseball history have the worst year of his career, batting just .254, with only ten home runs.

The big knocker on the Red Sox that year was outfielder Jackie Jensen, the league's RBI leader for the second straight time, with 112. Jensen hit 28 home runs and batted .277. The team's top average was compiled by Pete Runnels, the line drive-hitting second baseman, who turned in a .314 mark, as he warmed up for the batting title he would take the following season.

Firstbaseman Dick Gernert batted .262, while Boston's fine third baseman Frank Malzone checked in at .280, with 19 home runs and 92 RBIs, exactly the kind of year the team had been getting from Malzone since he took over at third in 1957. Until the blossoming of Wade Boggs in the 1980s, Malzone was considered by many to be the greatest thirdbaseman in Red Sox history. Behind the plate was nine year veteran Sammy White, in his final year with the club, batting .284. The 31-year-old White retired after the season,

The longer he was in baseball, the more popular Ted Williams became.

coming back a few years later to play briefly in the National League with the Braves and Phillies.

The Red Sox pitching consisted of an array of right-handers: Jerry Casale, Ike Delock, Tom Brewer, Frank Sullivan and Bill Monbouquette, with Casale the top winner at 13-8. This staff posted a rather high 4.17 ERA, and when the club led the league with 167 double plays, it led one wit to say, "Naturally. They always had a couple of men on base."

Jackie Jensen, American League RBI leader in 1959.

Pete Runnels. He batted .314 in 1959 and had batting championships coming up in 1960 and 1962.   *L.*

Frank Malzone.   *R.*

During a rain delay, some players were sitting around the clubhouse discussing fast ball pitchers. The name of Rex Barney, Brooklyn's extremely fast and very wild right-hander of the 1940s, was mentioned.

"He threw the ball like lightning," somebody said.

"Yes," said another. "Never twice in the same place."

NAME	G by POS	B	AGE	G	AB	R	H	2B	3B	HR	RBI	BB	SO	SB	BA	SA
BOSTON 5th 75-79 .487 19 PINKY HIGGINS 31-41 .425 RUDY YORK 0-1 .000 BILLY JURGES 44-36 .550																
TOTALS			29	154	5225	726	1335	248	28	125	671	626	810	68	.256	.385
Dick Gernert	1B75, OF25	R	30	117	298	41	78	14	1	11	42	52	49	1	.262	.426
Pete Runnels	2B101, 1B44, SS8	L	31	147	560	95	176	33	6	6	57	95	48	6	.314	.427
Don Buddin	SS150	R	25	151	485	75	117	24	1	10	53	92	99	6	.241	.357
Frank Malzone	3B154	R	29	154	604	90	169	34	2	19	92	42	58	6	.280	.437
Jackie Jensen	OF146	R	32	148	535	101	148	31	0	28	112	88	67	20	.277	.492
Gary Geiger	OF95	L	22	120	335	45	82	10	4	11	48	21	55	9	.245	.397
Ted Williams	OF76	L	40	103	272	32	69	15	0	10	43	52	27	0	.254	.419
Sammy White	C119	R	30	119	377	34	107	13	4	1	42	23	39	4	.284	.347
Marty Keough	OF69, 1B3	L	24	96	251	40	61	13	5	7	27	26	40	3	.243	.418
Vic Wertz	1B64	L	34	94	247	38	68	13	0	7	49	22	32	0	.275	.413
Gene Stephens (BA)	OF85	L	26	92	270	34	75	13	1	3	39	29	33	5	.278	.367
Pete Daley	C58	R	29	65	169	9	38	7	0	1	11	13	31	1	.225	.284
Jim Busby	OF34	R	32	61	102	16	23	8	0	1	5	5	18	0	.225	.333
Pumpsie Green	2B45, SS1	B	25	50	172	30	40	6	3	1	10	29	22	4	.233	.320
Jim Mahoney	SS30	R	25	31	23	10	3	0	0	1	3	7	0	.130	.261
2 Bobby Avila	2B11	R	35	22	45	7	11	0	0	3	6	6	11	0	.244	.444
Bill Renna	OF7	R	34	14	22	2	2	0	0	0	2	5	9	0	.091	.091
1 Billy Consolo 24 R 3-14, Jerry Mallett 23 R 4-15, Haywood Sullivan 28 R 0-2, 1 Ted Lepcio 28 R 1-3, Don Gile 24 R 2-10, 2 Herb Plews 31 L 1-12																

NAME	T	AGE	W	L	PCT	SV	G	GS	CG	IP	H	BB	SO	ShO	ERA
		27	75	79	.487	25	154	154	38	1364	1386	589	724	9	4.17
Jerry Casale	R	25	13	8	.619	0	31	26	9	180	162	89	93	3	4.30
Ike Delock	R	29	11	6	.647	0	28	17	4	134	120	62	55	0	2.96
Tom Brewer	R	27	10	12	.455	2	36	32	11	215	219	88	121	3	3.77
Frank Sullivan	R	29	9	11	.450	1	30	26	5	178	172	67	107	2	3.94
Bill Monbouquette	R	22	7	7	.500	0	34	17	4	152	165	33	87	0	4.14
Frank Baumann	L	26	6	4	.600	1	26	10	2	96	96	55	48	0	4.03
Mike Fornieles	R	27	5	3	.625	11	46	0	0	82	77	29	54	0	3.07
Nels Chittum	R	26	3	0	1.000	0	21	0	0	30	29	11	12	0	1.20
Leo Kiely	L	29	3	3	.500	7	41	0	0	56	67	18	30	0	4.18
2 Jack Harshman	L	31	2	3	.400	0	8	2	0	25	29	10	14	0	6.48
13 Murray Wall	R	32	2	5	.286	3	26	0	0	49	57	26	14	0	5.51
Ted Wills	L	25	2	6	.250	0	9	8	2	56	68	24	30	0	5.30
Earl Wilson	R	24	1	1	.500	0	9	4	0	24	21	31	17	0	6.00
2 Al Schroll	R	27	1	4	.200	0	14	5	1	46	47	22	26	0	4.70
Ted Bowsfield	L	23	0	1	.000	0	5	2	0	9	16	9	4	0	15.00
Herb Moford	R	30	0	2	.000	0	4	2	0	9	10	6	7	0	11.00
2 Billy Hoeft	L	27	0	3	.000	0	5	3	0	18	22	8	8	0	5.50
1 Dave Sisler	R	27	0	0	.000	0	3	0	0	7	9	1	3	0	6.43

Baltimore Orioles

The Orioles played better than .500 ball in each of the first two months of the season, but not again thereafter. Paul Richards' club puttered along throughout the summer, still as high as third place as late as August 26, but finally sinking into their eventual sixth-place finish, just five games out of third.

Richards, in the opinion of many an unrivaled handler of pitchers, got an exceptionally fine season out of knuckle-balling right-hander Hoyt Wilhelm. Converted by Richards into a starter, the long-time relief ace won his first nine games and wound up with a 15-11 record. Wilhelm's 2.19 ERA was the league's lowest.

Joining Wilhelm as a 15-game winner was 20-year-old Milt Pappas, who was 15-9. Baltimore's other starters were Skinny Brown (11-9), Jerry Walker (11-10) and left-hander Billy O'Dell (10-12). This staff delivered a league-high 15 shutouts (tied by the Yankees).

With Wilhelm in a starting role that year, Richards' number-one bullpen man was ex-Brooklyn Dodger Billy Loes. Loes, known in his Dodger days as moody and unpredictable, did passably well in his new role, winning four and saving 14.

Baltimore's .238 team batting average was seventh lowest in the league. What little offensive strength the club was able to mount came from veteran outfielder Gene Woodling (.300), outfielder Bob Nieman (.292, 21 homers) and catcher Gus Triandos, who batted a meager .216 but hit 25 home runs.

In his fifth year with the team was 22-year-old third baseman Brooks Robinson. Already the youngster's magical

Baltimore right-hander Milt Pappas. Just 20 years old in 1959, he was a 15-game winner. *L.*

Brooks Robinson. He batted .284 in 1959, but was so good with the glove that his pitchers said they didn't care if he never got a hit. *R.*

glove had earned him the respect of the opposition and the affectionate admiration of the Oriole pitchers. "We don't care if he never gets a hit," one of them said. It so happened that young Brooks was also earning his pay at home plate—he batted .284 that year.

First baseman Bob Boyd batted .265; shortstop Chico Carrasquel batted .223; and future Twins and Royals manager Billy Gardner batted only .217, which is just the kind of batting average that can turn a man's thoughts toward managing.

NAME	G by POS	B	AGE	G	AB	R	H	2B	3B	HR	RBI	BB	SO	SB	BA	SA
BALTIMORE 6th 74-80 .481 20							PAUL RICHARDS									
TOTALS			30	155	5208	551	1240	182	23	109	514	536	690	36	.238	.345
Bob Boyd	1B109	L	32	128	415	42	110	20	2	3	41	29	14	3	.265	.345
Billy Gardner	2B139,															
	3B1, SS12	R	31	140	401	34	87	13	2	6	27	38	61	2	.217	.304
Chico Carrasquel																
	SS89, 2B22, 3B2, 1B1	R	30	114	346	28	77	13	0	4	28	34	41	2	.223	.295
Brooks Robinson																
	3B87, 2B1	R	22	88	313	29	89	15	2	4	24	17	37	2	.284	.383
Gene Woodling	OF124	L	36	140	440	63	132	22	2	14	77	78	35	1	.300	.455
Willie Tasby	OF137	R	26	142	505	69	126	16	5	13	48	34	80	3	.250	.378
Bob Nieman	OF97	R	32	118	360	49	105	18	2	21	60	42	55	1	.292	.528
Gus Triandos	C125	R	28	126	393	43	85	7	1	25	73	65	56	0	.216	.430
Al Pilarcik	OF106	L	28	130	273	37	77	12	1	3	16	30	25	9	.282	.366
Billy Klaus	SS59,															
	3B49, 2B1	L	30	104	321	33	80	11	0	3	25	51	38	2	.249	.312
2 Albie Pearson	OF49	L	24	80	138	22	32	4	2	0	6	13	5	4	.232	.290
Joe Ginsberg	C62	L	32	65	166	14	30	2	0	1	14	21	13	1	.181	.211
Willie Miranda	SS47,															
	3B11, 2B5	B	33	65	88	8	14	5	0	0	7	7	18	0	.159	.216
2 Walt Dropo	1B54,															
	3B2	R	36	62	151	17	42	9	0	6	21	12	20	0	.278	.457
Jim Finigan	3B42, 2B6,															
	SS2	R	30	48	119	14	30	6	0	1	10	9	10	1	.252	.328
Bob Hale	1B8	L	25	40	54	2	10	3	0	0	7	2	6	0	.185	.241
1 Whitey Lockman																
	1B22, 2B5, OF1	L	32	38	69	7	15	1	1	0	2	8	4	0	.217	.261
Barry Shetrone	OF23	L	20	33	79	8	16	1	1	0	5	5	9	3	.203	.241
1 Lenny Green	OF23	L	25	27	24	3	7	0	0	1	2	1	3	0	.292	.417
1 Bobby Avila	OF10,															
	2B8, 3B1	R	35	20	47	1	8	0	0	0	0	4	5	0	.170	.170

Joe Taylor 33 L 5-32, Jerry Adair 22 R 11-35, Fred Valentine 24 B 6-10, Leo Burke 25 R 2-10,
Ron Hansen 21 R 0-4, Bob Saverine 18 B 0-0

NAME	T	AGE	W	L	PCT	SV	G	GS	CG	IP	H	BB	SO	ShO	ERA
		27	74	80	.481	30	155	155	45	1400	1290	476	735	15	3.56
Milt Pappas	R	20	15	9	.625	3	29	27	15	209	175	120	75	4	3.27
Hoyt Wilhelm	R	35	15	11	.577	0	32	27	13	226	178	77	139	3	2.19
Hal Brown	R	34	11	9	.550	3	31	21	2	164	158	32	81	0	3.79
Jerry Walker	R	20	11	10	.524	4	30	22	7	182	160	52	100	2	2.92
Billy O'Dell	L	26	10	12	.455	1	38	24	6	199	163	67	88	2	2.94
Ernie Johnson	R	35	4	1	.800	1	31	1	0	50	57	19	29	0	4.14
Billy Loes	R	29	4	7	.364	14	37	0	0	64	58	25	34	0	4.08
Arnie Portocarrero	R	27	2	7	.222	0	27	14	1	90	107	32	23	0	6.80
3 Billy Hoeft	L	27	1	1	.500	0	16	3	0	41	50	19	30	0	5.71
Jack Fisher	R	20	1	6	.143	2	27	7	1	89	76	38	52	1	3.03
George Zuverink (SJ)	R	34	0	1	.000	0	6	0	0	13	15	6	1	0	4.15
1 Jack Harshman	L	31	0	6	.000	0	14	8	0	47	58	28	24	0	6.89
Wes Stock	R	25	0	0	.000	1	7	0	0	13	16	2	8	0	3.46
2 Rip Coleman	L	27	0	0	.000	0	3	0	0	4	4	2	4	0	0.00
George Bamberger	R	33	0	0	.000	1	3	1	0	8	15	2	2	0	7.88

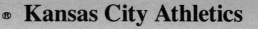# Kansas City Athletics

Forty-five players were employed by the Kansas City Athletics in 1959, playing from one game to a full season. Of these forty-five, at least twenty had already been, or shortly would be, employed by the Yankees. The trading shuttle between New York and Kansas City in those years, with all of KC's most talented players going East, was scandalously reminiscent of the rape of the Red Sox after the first World War, when Yankee cash kept a steady stream of Red Sox stars coming to New York.

Harry Craft's club played .500 ball until the end of July, then took a complete nosedive in August and September, winning 16 and losing 38. It was their third-straight seventh-place finish.

Craft's most talented player, outfielder Roger Maris, missed 30 games because of injuries and was held to a .273 batting average and 16 home runs. The Yankees, however, were enamored of Roger's smooth left-handed stroke, and on December 11, Maris, first baseman Kent Hadley and short-stop Joe DeMaestri were traded to the Yankees. The Athletics received: outfielder Hank Bauer, who was washed-up; pitcher Don Larsen, who was over the hill; first baseman Marv Throneberry, who was indescribably inept; and outfielder Norm Siebern, a fine player. Maris was the MVP in 1960 and again in 1961, when he broke Babe Ruth's single-season home run record.

The A's had one .300 hitter in outfielder Bill Tuttle, who hit it on the nose, while ex-Yankee Bob Cerv (he would be re-summoned to New York the following year) batted .285 and hit 20 home runs. The club also had a pair of future heavy-

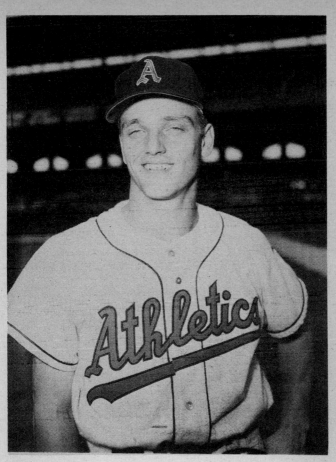

Kansas City outfielder Roger Maris, who was traded to the Yankees after the season.

duty players in its ranks that year: utility man Dick Williams got into 130 games at four positions and batted .266, while outfielder Whitey Herzog got into 38 games and batted .293.

Left-hander Bud Daley, a 16-game winner for the lowly Kansas City Athletics in 1959.

Left-hander Bud Daley was the team's top winner, with a 16-13 record (they punched his ticket to New York in 1961). Ray Hebert was 11-11 and Ned Garver 10-13.

NAME	G by POS	B	AGE	G	AB	R	H	2B	3B	HR	RBI	BB	SO	SB	BA	SA
KANSAS CITY 7th 66-88 .429 28								HARRY CRAFT								
TOTALS			28	154	5264	681	1383	231	43	117	638	481	780	34	.263	.390
Kent Hadley	1B95	L	24	113	288	40	73	11	1	10	39	24	74	1	.253	.403
Wayne Terwilliger 2B63, SS2, 3B1		R	34	74	180	27	48	11	0	2	18	19	31	2	.267	.361
Joe DeMaestri SS115 3B80,		R	30	118	352	31	86	16	5	6	34	28	65	1	.244	.369
Dick Williams 1B32, OF23, 2B3		R	30	130	488	72	130	33	1	16	75	28	60	4	.266	.436
Roger Maris (IL)	OF117	L	24	122	433	69	118	21	7	16	72	58	53	2	.273	.464
Bill Tuttle	OF121	R	29	126	463	74	139	19	6	7	43	48	38	10	.300	.413
Bob Cerv	OF119	R	33	125	463	61	132	22	4	20	87	35	87	3	.285	.479
Frank House	C95	L	29	98	347	32	82	14	3	1	30	20	23	0	.236	.303
2 Jerry Lumpe 2B61, SS56, 3B4		L	26	108	403	47	98	11	5	3	28	41	32	2	.243	.318
Hal Smith 3B77, C22		R	28	108	292	36	84	12	0	5	31	34	39	0	.288	.380
Russ Snyder	OF64	L	25	73	243	41	76	13	2	3	21	19	29	6	.313	.420
2 Ray Boone 1B38, 3B3		R	35	61	132	19	36	6	0	2	12	27	17	1	.273	.364
Preston Ward 1B22, OF1		L	31	58	109	8	27	4	1	2	19	7	12	0	.248	.358
Harry Chiti	C47	R	26	55	162	20	44	11	1	6	25	17	26	0	.272	.444
Zeke Bella	OF25, 1B1	R	28	47	82	10	17	2	1	1	9	9	14	0	.207	.293
Bud Daley	P39	L	26	39	78	5	23	1	0	0	13	2	11	0	.295	.308
Whitey Herzog (IL) OF34, 1B1		L	27	38	123	25	36	7	1	1	9	34	23	1	.293	.390
1 Hector Lopez	2B33	R	26	35	135	22	38	10	3	6	24	8	23	1	.281	.533
Ned Garver	P32	R	33	32	71	9	20	2	1	2	9	4	7	0	.282	.423
2 Ray Jablonski	3B17	R	32	25	65	4	17	1	0	2	8	3	11	0	.262	.369
Joe Morgan	3B2	L	28	20	21	2	4	0	1	0	3	3	7	0	.190	.286
Lou Klimchock	2B16	L	19	17	66	10	18	1	0	4	13	1	6	0	.273	.470
Tommy Carroll 22 R 1-7, 1 Harry Simpson 33 L 4-14, Bob Martyn 28 L 0-1																

NAME	T	AGE	W	L	PCT	SV	G	GS	CG	IP	H	BB	SO	ShO	ERA
		30	66	88	.429	21	154	154	44	1361	1452	492	703	8	4.35
Bud Daley	L	26	16	13	.552	1	39	29	12	216	212	62	125	2	3.17
Ray Herbert	R	29	11	11	.500	1	37	26	10	184	196	62	99	2	4.84
Ned Garver	R	33	10	13	.435	1	32	20	9	201	214	42	61	2	3.72
2 Johnny Kucks	R	25	8	11	.421	1	33	23	6	151	163	42	51	1	3.87
Bob Grim	R	29	6	10	.375	4	40	9	3	125	124	57	65	1	4.10
John Tsitouris	R	23	4	3	.571	0	24	10	0	83	90	35	50	0	4.99
Murry Dickson	R	42	2	1	.667	0	38	0	0	71	85	27	36	0	4.94
1 Ralph Terry	R	23	2	4	.333	0	9	7	2	46	56	19	35	0	5.28
2 Tom Sturdivant	R	29	2	6	.250	5	36	3	0	72	70	34	57	0	4.63
1 Rip Coleman	L	27	2	10	.167	2	29	11	2	81	85	34	54	0	4.56
Russ Meyer	R	35	1	0	1.000	1	18	0	0	24	24	11	10	0	4.50
Tom Gorman	R	34	1	0	1.000	1	17	0	0	20	24	14	9	0	7.20
Ken Johnson	R	26	1	1	.500	0	2	2	0	11	11	5	8	0	4.09
Dick Tomanek	L	28	0	1	.000	2	16	0	0	21	27	12	13	0	6.43
Al Grunwald	L	29	0	1	.000	1	6	1	0	11	18	11	9	0	8.18
Howie Reed	R	22	0	3	.000	0	6	3	0	21	26	10	11	0	7.29
Evans Killeen	R	23	0	0	.000	0	4	0	0	6	4	4	1	0	4.50
Marty Kutyna	R	26	0	0	.000	1	4	0	0	7	7	1	1	0	8.00
2 Mark Freeman	R	28	0	0	.000	0	3	0	0	4	6	3	1	0	9.00
George Brunet	L	24	0	0	.000	0	2	0	0	5	10	7	7	0	10.80

Washington Senators

Manager Cookie Lavagetto's Washington Senators finished in last place for the third year in a row in 1959, 31 games behind the first-place White Sox. In spite of this gloomy season, the team had some fine players who enjoyed productive years. Tying for the league home-run lead (with Rocky Colavito) was 23-year-old third baseman Harmon Killebrew. Playing his first full season, the Idaho strongboy clouted 42 home runs and drove in 105 runs, though batting only .242 (Killebrew never hit for high averages). He was only the second Washington player ever to lead the league in home runs, Roy Sievers having been the first, in 1957.

Sievers was still with the Senators, playing first base and hitting 21 home runs. He was part of one of the most powerful slugging units in the league, a group whose longball exploits belied the team's dismal finish. Outfielder Jim Lemon hit 33 homers and drove in 100 runs, and Rookie-of-the-Year Bob Allison cracked 30 one-way shots. Allison's selection, after Albie Pearson's in 1958, made it two Rookies-of-the-Year in a row for the Senators.

In spite of all the thunder, the team scored only 619 runs, seventh lowest in the league (their 163 home runs ranked second to Cleveland's 167), while their .237 batting average was the league's worst, as were their 162 errors.

The power swing of Harmon Killebrew.　　　*Opposite, Top*

Camilo Pascual.　　　*Opposite, bot. L.*

Bob Allison, Washington's power-hitting Rookie of the Year in 1959.　　　*Opposite, bot. R.*

Washington's Jim Lemon.

of the club's better stickmen, with a batting average of .251.

On the mound, Lavagetto had two fine assets in right-handers Camilo Pascual and Pedro Ramos. Pascual, for years one of the league's premier pitchers, was 17-10, with a league-leading six shutouts, while Ramos was 13-19.

The weak-hitting Senators that year included infielders Reno Bertoia (.237), Billy Consolo (.213), Ron Samford (.224) and Ken Aspromonte (.244). Catcher Hal Naragon was at .241 and another catcher, Clint Courtney hit .233. Outfielder Faye Throneberry, older brother of Marv, was one

NAME	G by POS	B	AGE	G	AB	R	H	2B	3B	HR	RBI	BB	SO	SB	BA	SA
WASHINGTON 8th 63-91 .409 31							COOKIE LAVAGETTO									
TOTALS			27	154	5092	619	1205	173	32	163	579	517	881	51	.237	.379
Roy Sievers	1B93, OF13	R	32	115	385	55	93	19	0	21	49	53	62	1	.242	.455
Reno Bertoia	2B71, 3B5, SS1	R	24	90	308	33	73	10	0	8	29	29	48	2	.237	.347
2 Billy Consolo	SS75, 2B4	R	24	79	202	25	43	5	3	0	10	36	54	1	.213	.267
Harmon Killebrew	3B150, OF4	R	23	153	546	98	132	20	2	42	105	90	116	3	.242	.516
Faye Throneberry	OF86	L	28	117	327	36	82	11	2	10	42	33	61	6	.251	.388
Bob Allison	OF149	R	24	150	570	83	149	18	9	30	85	60	92	13	.261	.482
Jim Lemon	OF142	R	31	147	531	73	148	18	3	33	100	46	99	5	.279	.510
2 Hal Naragon	C54	L	30	71	195	12	47	3	2	0	11	8	9	0	.241	.277
Julio Becquer	1B53	L	27	108	220	20	59	12	5	1	26	8	17	3	.268	.382
Ron Samford	SS64, 2B23	R	29	91	237	23	53	13	0	5	22	11	29	1	.224	.342
2 Lenny Green	OF58	L	25	88	190	29	46	6	1	2	15	20	15	9	.242	.316
Clint Courtney (IL)	C63	L	32	72	189	19	44	4	1	2	18	20	19	0	.233	.296
Ken Aspromonte	2B52, SS12, 1B1, OF1	R	27	70	225	31	55	12	0	2	14	26	39	2	.244	.324
1 Jay Porter	C34, 1B2	R	26	37	106	8	24	4	0	1	10	11	16	0	.226	.292
Camilo Pascual	P32	R	25	32	86	10	26	2	0	0	3	5	11	0	.302	.326
Zoilo Versalles	SS29	R	19	29	59	4	9	0	0	1	1	4	15	1	.153	.203
1 Herb Plews	2B6	L	31	27	40	4	9	0	0	0	2	3	5	0	.225	.225
1 Albie Pearson	OF22	L	24	25	80	9	15	1	0	0	2	14	3	1	.188	.200
Josie Valdivielso	SS21	R	25	24	14	1	4	0	0	0	0	1	3	0	.286	.286
1 Ed Fitz Gerald	C16	R	35	19	62	5	12	3	0	0	5	4	8	0	.194	.242
Norm Zauchin	1B19	R	29	19	71	11	15	4	0	3	4	7	14	2	.211	.394

Steve Korcheck 26 R 8-51, Dan Dobbek 24 L 15-60, Johnny Schaive 25 R 9-59, Bobby Malkmus 27 R 0-0

NAME	T	AGE	W	L	PCT	SV	G	GS	CG	IP	H	BB	SO	ShO	ERA
		25	63	91	.409	21	154	154	46	1360	1358	457	694	10	4.01
Camilo Pascual	R	25	17	10	.630	0	32	30	17	238	202	69	185	6	2.64
Pedro Ramos	R	24	13	18	.406	0	37	35	11	234	233	52	95	0	4.15
Bill Fischer	R	28	9	11	.450	0	34	29	6	187	211	43	62	1	4.28
Tex Clevenger	R	26	8	5	.615	8	50	7	2	117	114	51	71	2	3.92
Russ Kemmerer	R	27	8	17	.320	0	37	28	8	206	221	71	89	0	4.50
Hal Woodeschick	L	26	2	4	.333	0	31	3	0	61	58	36	30	0	3.69
Dick Hyde (SA)	R	30	2	5	.286	4	37	0	0	54	56	27	29	0	5.00
Hal Griggs	R	30	2	8	.200	2	37	10	2	98	103	52	43	1	5.23
John Romonosky	R	29	1	0	1.000	0	12	2	0	38	36	19	22	0	3.32
Chuck Stobbs	L	29	1	8	.111	7	41	7	0	91	82	24	50	0	2.87
Vito Valentinetti	R	30	0	2	.000	0	7	1	0	11	16	10	7	0	10.92
Jim Kaat	L	20	0	2	.000	0	3	2	0	5	7	4	2	0	12.00
Jack Kralick	L	24	0	0	.000	0	6	0	0	12	13	6	7	0	7.75
Ralph Lumenti	L	22	0	0	.000	0	2	0	0	3	2	1	2	0	0.00
2 Murray Wall	R	33	0	0	.000	0	1	0	0	1	3	0	0	0	8.00
Tom McAvoy	L	22	0	0	.000	0	1	0	0	3	1	2	0	0	0.00

The World Series

The first World Series ever played on the West Coast was won by the Los Angeles Dodgers in six games over the Chicago White Sox. The White Sox, however, started the Series with a bang, scoring a thundering 11-0 win in the opener at Comiskey Park.

The White Sox scored two in the bottom of the first against Roger Craig, then tore the game apart with seven runs in the bottom of the third, highlighted by a three-run homer from Ted Kluszewski. Early Wynn went the first seven, then moved aside for Gerry Staley, who completed the shutout. The Sox' final two runs came on another Kluszewski blast in the fourth.

In Game 2, the Dodgers were trailing, 2-1, in the top of the seventh when, with two out, they suddenly ambushed White Sox starter Bob Shaw. Pinch-hitter Chuck Essegian tied it with a home run; Jim Gilliam walked, and then Charlie Neal, who had earlier homered for the Dodgers' first run, belted another. Larry Sherry, who took over for Johnny Podres in the last of the seventh, went the rest of the way, giving up a run in the eighth but holding on for a 4-3 win.

The Series then moved to Los Angeles, where the next three games drew tremendous, record-shattering crowds into the sun-baked Coliseum. Game three had 92,394 paying customers in attendance. After Dick Donovan and Don Drysdale had dueled for six scoreless innings, the Dodgers scored a couple in the bottom of the seventh. With two out and Neal on second, Donovan walked Norm Larker and Gil Hodges, filling the bases. Staley replaced Donovan and Carl Furillo was sent up to hit for Don Demeter. The old Ebbets Field hero

Ted Kluszewski. After a long career in the National League, the big muscle man finally made it to the World Series with the White Sox.   *L.*

Chuck Essegian, who set a record by pinch-hitting two home runs for the Dodgers in the 1959 World Series. Behind Chuck is the Los Angeles Memorial Coliseum. There was no protection from the broiling southern California sun for the fans in the bleachers.   *R.*

responded with a two-run single. Sherry replaced Drysdale in the eighth, as the Sox scored once. The Dodgers made it 3-1 in the last of the eighth, and Sherry fanned the side in the ninth for his second save.

The Dodgers made it three games to one the next day (before 92, 650 fans) by a 5-4 score. With the game tied, 4-4, in the last of the eighth, Hodges sent a home run into the left-field stands. Wynn and Craig had started, but the winner for

Bob Shaw, who pitched brilliantly for the White Sox in the fifth game of the World Series.   *L.*

Wally Moon.   *R.*

the Dodgers was the ubiquitous Sherry (who had come on in the top of the eighth), while the loss went to Staley.

In the fifth game, before 92,706 fans, the White Sox stayed alive, thanks to the air-tight pitching of Shaw ($7^1/3$ innings), Billy Pierce (one batter) and Dick Donovan ($1^2/3$ innings). They outdueled Sandy Koufax (seven innings) and Stan Williams (two innings) in a 1-0 beauty. The game's only run was scored in the top of the fourth on singles by Nelson Fox and Jim Landis, and a double-play grounder by Sherman Lollar. It was a frustrating afternoon for the Dodgers, who had nine hits and left 11 men on base.

The Series returned to Chicago for game six and there the Dodgers wrapped it up early. At the end of four innings,

Action from the 1959 World Series. The Dodgers' Maury Wills is defending against a steal attempt by the White Sox' Luis Aparicio. Luis was safe. The play occurred in the first inning of Game 4.

Alston's squad led, 8-3, thanks to six runs in the fourth. The Dodgers devastated starter Wynn and then reliever Turk

Lown. Duke Snider and Wally Moon blasted key home runs.

When Dodger starter Johnny Podres weakened in the last of the fourth, giving up three runs (including Kluszewski's third homer of the Series), Sherry came in to fire $5^2/3$ scoreless innings, gaining his second Series win to go along with his two saves. In the top of the ninth, Essegian set a World Series record when he pinch-hit his second home run of the October pageant. The final score was 9-3.

The hitting stars for the Dodgers were Neal, with 10 hits and a .370 average, and Hodges, with 9 hits and a .391 average. Snider's home run was his eleventh in Series competition, which at the time tied him with Mickey Mantle in second place to Babe Ruth's 15. (Mantle eventually hit 18 to lead everyone.)

Kluszewski was the single biggest gun for the White Sox, with nine hits, including three homers, a .391 average and 10 runs batted in, still the record for a six-game Series.

With no pitcher going the distance, the mound star was easily Sherry, with his two wins, two saves and 0.71 ERA for $12^2/3$ innings. Also crucial to the Dodgers' victory was the strong throwing arm of catcher John Roseboro, who stopped—by deed and with intimidation—the Sox' vaunted running game, holding team to just two stolen bases.

The 1959 World Series

LINE SCORES

TEAM	1	2	3	4	5	6	7	8	9	10	11	12	R	H	E
Game 1 October 1 at Chicago															
LA (NL)	0	0	0	0	0	0	0	0	0				0	8	3
CHI (AL)	2	0	7	2	0	0	0	0	X				11	11	0
Craig, Churn (3), Labine (4), Koufax (5), Klippstein (7)						Wynn, Staley (8)									
Game 2 October 2 at Chicago															
LA	0	0	0	0	1	0	3	0	0				4	9	1
CHI	2	0	0	0	0	0	0	1	0				3	8	0
Padres, Sherry (3)						Shaw, Lown (7)									
Game 3 October 4 at Los Angeles															
CHI	0	0	0	0	0	0	0	1	0				1	12	0
LA	0	0	0	0	0	0	2	1	X				3	5	0
Donovan, Staley (7)						Drysdale, Sherry (8)									
Game 4 October 5 at Los Angeles															
CHI	0	0	0	0	0	0	4	0	0				4	10	3
LA	0	0	4	0	0	0	0	1	X				5	9	0
Wynn, Lown (3), Pierce (4), Staley (7)						Craig, Sherry (8)									
Game 5 October 6 at Los Angeles															
CHI	0	0	0	1	0	0	0	0	0				1	5	0
LA	0	0	0	0	0	0	0	0	0				0	9	0
Shaw, Pierce (8), Donovan (8)						Koufax, Williams (8)									
Game 6 October 8 at Chicago															
LA	0	0	2	6	0	0	0	0	1				9	13	0
CHI	0	0	0	3	0	0	0	0	0				3	6	1
Padres, Sherry (4)						Wynn, Donovan (4), Lown (4), Staley (5), Pierce (8), Moore (9)									

World Series
Los Angeles (NL) 4
Chicago (AL) 2

COMPOSITE BATTING

NAME	POS	G	AB	R	H	2B	3B	HR	RBI	BA
Los Angeles (NL)										
TOTALS		6	203	21	53	3	1	7	19	.261
Neal	2B	6	27	4	10	2	0	2	6	.370
Gilliam	3B	6	25	2	6	0	0	0	0	.240
Hodges	1B	6	23	2	9	0	1	1	2	.391
Moon	OF	6	23	3	6	0	0	1	2	.261
Roseboro	C	6	21	0	2	0	0	0	1	.095
Wills	SS	6	20	2	5	0	0	0	1	.250
Larker	OF	6	16	2	3	0	0	0	0	.188
Demeter	OF	6	12	2	3	0	0	0	0	.250
Snider	OF	4	10	1	2	0	0	1	2	.200
Sherry	P	5	4	0	2	0	0	0	0	.500
Podres	P	3	4	1	2	1	0	0	1	.500
Furillo	OF	4	4	0	1	0	0	0	2	.250
Essegian	PH	4	3	2	2	0	0	2	2	.667
Fairly	OF	6	3	0	0	0	0	0	0	.000
Craig	P	2	3	0	0	0	0	0	0	.000
Koufax	P	2	2	0	0	0	0	0	0	.000
Drysdale	P	1	2	0	0	0	0	0	0	.000
Zimmer	SS	1	1	0	0	0	0	0	0	.000
Pignatano	C	1	0	0	0	0	0	0	0	.000
Repulski	PH	1	0	0	0	0	0	0	0	.000
Churn P 0-0, Labine P 0-0, Klippstein P 0-0, Williams P 0-0										
Chicago (AL)										
TOTALS		6	199	23	52	10	0	4	19	.261
Aparicio	SS	6	26	1	8	1	0	0	0	.308
Fox	2B	6	24	4	9	3	0	0	0	.375
Landis	OF	6	24	6	7	0	0	0	1	.292
Kluszewski	1B	6	23	5	9	1	0	3	18	.391
Lollar	C	6	22	3	5	0	0	1	5	.227
Smith	OF	6	20	1	5	3	0	0	1	.250
Goodman	3B	5	13	1	3	0	0	0	1	.231
Rivera	OF	5	11	1	0	0	0	0	0	.000
Phillips	3B-OF	3	10	0	3	1	0	0	0	.300
Wynn	P	3	5	0	1	1	0	0	1	.200
McAnany	OF	3	5	0	0	0	0	0	0	.000
Shaw	P	2	4	0	1	0	0	0	0	.250
Cash	PH	4	4	0	0	0	0	0	0	.000
Donovan	P	3	3	0	1	0	0	0	0	.333
Esposito	3B	2	2	0	0	0	0	0	0	.000
Torgeson	1B	3	1	1	0	0	0	0	0	.000
Romano	PH	2	1	0	0	0	0	0	0	.000
Staley	P	4	1	0	0	0	0	0	0	.000
Lown P 0-0, Pierce P 0-0, Moore P 0-0										

COMPOSITE PITCHING

NAME	G	IP	H	BB	SO	W	L	SV	ERA
Los Angeles (NL)									
TOTALS	6	53	52	20	33	4	2	2	3.23
Sherry	4	12.2	8	2	5	2	0	2	6.71
Podres	2	9.1	7	6	4	1	0	0	4.82
Craig	2	9.1	15	5	8	0	1	0	8.68
Koufax	2	9	5	1	7	0	1	0	1.00
Drysdale	1	7	11	4	5	1	0	0	1.29
Williams	1	2	0	2	1	0	0	0	0.00
Klippstein	1	2	1	0	2	0	0	0	0.00
Labine	1	1	0	0	1	0	0	0	0.00
Churn	1	.2	5	0	0	0	0	0	27.00
Chicago (AL)									
TOTALS	6	52	53	12	27	2	4	2	3.46
Shaw	2	14	17	2	2	1	1	0	2.57
Wynn	3	13	19	4	10	1	1	0	5.54
Staley	4	8.1	8	0	3	0	1	1	2.16
Donovan	3	8.1	4	3	5	0	1	1	5.40
Pierce	3	4	2	2	3	0	0	0	0.00
Lown	3	3.1	2	1	3	0	0	0	0.00
Moore	1	1	1	0	1	0	0	0	9.00

1959 Final Standings

National League

Club	Won	Lost	Pct.	GB
Los Angeles	88	68	.564	—
Milwaukee	86	70	.551	2
San Francisco	83	71	.539	4
Pittsburgh	78	76	.506	9
Chicago	74	80	.481	13
Cincinnati	74	80	.481	13
St. Louis	71	83	.461	16
Philadelphia	64	90	.416	23

American League

Chicago	94	60	.610	—
Cleveland	89	65	.578	5
New York	79	75	.513	15
Detroit	76	78	.494	18
Boston	75	79	.487	19
Baltimore	74	80	.481	20
Kansas City	66	88	.429	28
Washington	63	91	.409	31

1959 All-Star Games

For the first time since its inception in 1933, the annual All-Star Game was turned into a double feature. The reason for adding a second game of the stars was to generate additional funding for the players' pension fund, for youthful baseball and for assisting needy former players.

With the squads then being selected by a poll of players, coaches, and managers (no one was permitted to vote for a player on his own club), the games were scheduled for Pittsburgh's Forbes Field on July 7, and Los Angeles' Memorial Coliseum on August 3.

The first game was won by the National League, 5-4. Eddie Mathews homered for the National side and Al Kaline for the American. Willie Mays, always a scintillating All-Star Game performer, drove in the winning run with a triple in the last of the eighth.

The second game went to the American League, 5-3. Five home runs were hit: Frank Malzone, Yogi Berra and Rocky Colavito for the American League, and Frank Robinson and Jim Gilliam for the National.

Red Sox third-baseman Frank Malzone, who homered for the American League in 1959's second All-Star Game.

Rocky Colavito's
Four Home Runs

On June 10, 1959, Cleveland's Rocky Colavito turned in an explosive batting performance that earned him a place among the game's slugging elite. Not only did the big right-handed batter hit four home runs in a single game in successive at-bats, but he achieved the rare feat in Baltimore's Memorial Stadium, where the generous outfield dimensions made it the major's most difficult park for homers.

Rocky was only the second American Leaguer to connect four times in a single game (Lou Gehrig had done it in 1932); and only two National Leaguers had homered four times in a nine-inning game in the 20th century—Gil Hodges in 1950, and Joe Adcock in 1954.

On his first at-bat, in the first inning, Colavito walked, and then in the third, fifth, sixth and ninth innings he homered. For the night, he was four-for-four, driving in six runs in Cleveland's 11-8 victory.

Further underlining Colavito's achievement was the fact that before this game no *team* had ever hit more than three home runs in a single game in the Baltimore ball park. Joining Rocky in the home run circle that night were teammates Minnie Miñoso and Billy Martin (yes, that Billy Martin).

Rocky Colavito entered the record books on June 10, 1959.

Harvey Haddix' Perfect Game

On May 26, 1959, Pittsburgh's Harvey Haddix pitched the greatest game in baseball history—and lost. How do you lose a perfect game? Well, the secret is to keep pitching it long enough. That is what Haddix did against Lew Burdette and a heavy-hitting Milwaukee lineup (which included Henry Aaron, Eddie Mathews, and Joe Adcock).

Haddix retired the first 27 men he faced, but Burdette, who surrendered 12 hits over the course of the evening, was also pitching shutout ball. Haddix retired three more men in a row in the tenth, the eleventh, and then the twelfth. (No other pitcher had ever pitched more than $10^{2/3}$ hitless innings in a game.)

He knew that he had a no-hitter, Haddix said, but he didn't know about the perfect game. In the bottom of the thirteenth, it all went by the boards—the perfect game, the no-hitter, the shutout, the game itself.

Felix Mantilla led off by grounding to Don Hoak at third; Hoak fielded the ball cleanly, but threw low to first, the error enabling Mantilla to become the first Milwaukee base runner. Mathews bunted Mantilla to second. Aaron was intentionally walked. Adcock then hit a drive over the center-field fence. Because of a base-running mistake by Aaron, the blow counted only as a double. But it was enough to give the Braves a 1-0 victory and make a loser of Haddix, the man who had pitched the greatest game in baseball history.

Harvey Haddix pitching to Eddie Mathews during Harvey's historic performance on May 26, 1959.

A New Strikeout Record

The Dodgers' 23-year-old Sandy Koufax, soon to burst upon the baseball universe with unparalleled brilliance, gave a compelling demonstration of what was imminent in the game he pitched against the San Francisco Giants on August 31, 1959.

Facing a lineup that included Willie Mays, Willie McCovey, Orlando Cepeda, and Felipe Alou, Koufax broke Dizzy Dean's 1933 National League record of 17 strikeouts and tied Bob Feller's major league record of 18.

Sandy Koufax.

In pitching the Dodgers to a 5-2 victory (won by Wally Moon's three-run homer in the bottom of the ninth), Koufax kept getting better and better as the game went along. Starting with one out in the fourth inning, 15 of his last 17 outs were achieved via strikeouts.

"He was throwing faster in the ninth than he was in the first," Walter Alston said. "Much, much faster. I know that's hard to believe, but, then again, so was Koufax. He was that good."

Koufax walked two and gave up seven hits, including a home run to McCovey. The young lefty fanned McCovey, Mays and Cepeda twice each and Alou once.

For today's fans, a doubleheader is a rare occasion, almost always being the result of a rain-out earlier in the season. In 1959, however, the two-for-one event was a regular attraction in the schedule. The Cleveland Indians played 24 doubleheaders that year, more than any other club. They won nine, lost five and split ten. But the doubleheader champs that year were the pennant-winning White Sox, who won ten, lost three and split eight. At the opposite end of the scale were the Washington Senators, whose 91 losses were the most in baseball that year. They won a single doubleheader, lost seven and split nine.

Coming Attractions

Baseball is the game that never disappoints.

No matter how lopsided the score, the perceptive fan can always find something to concentrate on and appreciate, be it a defensive play, the taking of an extra base by a joyously unleashed base runner, or some subtle conflict of wills between pitcher and batter. And there is another area in which baseball, from its very beginnings, has never disappointed: the production of star players.

It is almost as if there is a manufacturing plant somewhere, containing designers and artisans of varying skill and imagination, each charged with the task of producing something quite unlike anything that has gone before. In the real world of organized baseball, these plants are called the minor leagues, best remembered by their employees for long bus rides, meager salaries, wretched playing surfaces, inadequate lighting, often no dugouts, sometimes no showers. By some they are remembered as times of hope and dreams, of expectations that lay far beyond the unpainted fences of small-town playing fields. When you are young and strong and fleet of foot and—maybe—talented, it is your right and even your obligation to dream; and young ballplayers have only the one dream, the one that muscles them forward and enables them to tolerate the uncertainties and the discomforts: the big leagues.

The minor leagues reached their peak in the years immediately following World War II, when there were nearly 60 of these circuits scattered around the country. By 1959, there were just 21. So the opportunities were fewer, the competition more intense; but still the dreams swelled and billowed with the same freedom and audacity as ever. In 1959, the stars that baseball never ceases producing were being honed and polished at one level or other of the game's production structure.

Pitching for Omaha of the American Association in 1959 was right-hander Bob Gibson, in his third year of pro ball. The fast-baller was 9-9 before being brought up by the Cardinals in midseason.

Playing in his second year of pro ball for Springfield, Massachusetts, in the Eastern League was another young right-hander of future distinction, Juan Marichal. Marichal, whose Hall of Fame career would parallel that of Gibson's, turned in an 18-13 record that year, and his high-kicking delivery had already caught the attention of the San Francisco Giants' front office, who would bring him to the top late in the 1960 season.

Recipient of a $108,000 signing bonus from the Los Angeles Dodgers, the 6'7", 250-pound Frank Howard ("It was like pitching to a building," one pitcher said) was hitting home runs that disappeared into the clouds, first for Victoria in the Texas League and later Spokane in the Pacific Coast League.

Raleigh, North Carolina, in the Carolina League had the league's leading hitter in a young man destined to ornament Boston's Fenway Park for the next two decades. His name was Carl Yastrzemski, and in 1959 he machine-gunned Carolina League pitching for a .377 batting average, more than 50 points better than the runner-up.

Willie Davis, who would sparkle in the Los Angeles Dodger outfield for a decade and collect over 2,000 major league hits, played for Reno, Nevada, in the California League and batted .365 to run away with the batting crown.

Carl Yastrzemski. In 1959, he was wowin' 'em in the Carolina League.

Scattered throughout the minor-league systems were others who realized the dream and reached the major leagues, some briefly, some for modest careers, a few others for stardom. But most of the approximately 3,000 young men playing professional baseball in the year 1959 never made it to the top. It was the survival of the few; the best ultimately had to compete with the best. If your bat was a bit slow or your eye-hand coordination was not up to dealing with the curve, or your fast ball was too slow, or your breaking ball no mystery, or your arm too weak or your legs too heavy, one day soon someone would put his arm around your shoulders and in a soft voice tell you some bad news.

Grand-Slam Home Runs

It's the biggest bang-for-the-buck in baseball, the one swing of the bat that can net your team four runs at once. It's part of baseball's democratic purity in that you can be the smallest guy on the team, the weakest hitter, and still hit one out with the bases loaded, or, as the writers are wont to say, the sacks filled, the bags bulging, a man on every base. It's the time when the manager walks out to the mound and has a sublime comment on the obvious: "You're in trouble." One story has a manager going out to his pitcher in this dire situation and telling him, "Now watch it, the bases are loaded," and the pitcher (they are never in good humor under these circumstances) saying, "I know. I didn't think I had a second infield."

There were 52 "jackpot shots" hit in the major leagues in 1959, 29 by the American League, 23 by the National. Detroit right-hander Ray Narleski was the most generous dispenser of baseball's most shuddering shot, being roughed up four times in the course of the season.

Following is a list, by league, of the players who clouted four-run four-baggers in 1959:

American League

Apr. 14:	Bill Skowron, New York	vs. Baltimore
Apr. 14:	Woodie Held, Cleveland	vs. Detroit
Apr. 15:	Bob Grim, Kansas City	vs. Chicago
Apr. 21:	Gus Triandos, Baltimore	vs. Boston
May 2:	Jim Lemon, Washington	vs. Detroit
May 5:	Ted Lepcio, Detroit	vs. Boston
May 6:	Bob Allison, Washington	vs. Chicago

May 20:	Eddie Yost, Detroit	vs. New York
May 31:	Preston Ward, Kansas City	vs. Chicago
June 13:	Rocky Colavito, Cleveland	vs. Washington
June 14:	Minnie Miñoso, Cleveland	vs. Washington
June 25:	Rocky Bridges, Detroit	vs. Boston
June 26:	Jackie Jensen, Boston	vs. Cleveland
June 27:	Harry Simpson, Chicago	vs. New York
July 2:	Charlie Maxwell, Detroit	vs. Chicago
July 2:	Al Smith, Chicago	vs. Detroit
July 3:	Bob Cerv, Kansas City	vs. Cleveland
July 11:	Don Buddin, Boston	vs. New York
July 13:	Gene Stephens, Boston	vs. New York
July 23:	Minnie Miñoso, Cleveland	vs. New York
July 27:	Faye Throneberry, Washington	vs. Kansas City
July 27:	Gene Woodling, Baltimore	vs. Detroit
July 27:	Roger Maris, Kansas City	vs. Washington
Aug. 14:	Vic Wertz, Boston	vs. New York (pinch hit)
Aug. 22:	Woodie Held, Cleveland	vs. Baltimore
Aug. 23:	Eddie Yost, Detroit	vs. Baltimore
Aug. 24:	Gus Triandos, Baltimore	vs. Detroit
Sept. 5:	Jim Lemon, Washington	vs. Boston
Sept. 26:	Johnny Callison, Chicago	vs. Detroit

National League

Apr. 18:	Gene Freese, Philadelphia	vs. Cincinnati (pinch hit)
Apr. 24:	Eddie Mathews, Milwaukee	vs. Cincinnati
Apr. 26:	Dick Groat, Pittsburgh	vs. Philadelphia
May 9:	Ken Boyer, St. Louis	vs. Chicago
May 12:	Earl Averill, Chicago	vs. Milwaukee (pinch hit)
May 13:	Ernie Banks, Chicago	vs. Cincinnati

May 26:	Leon Wagner, San Francisco	vs. Los Angeles (pinch hit)
May 31:	Bob Skinner, Pittsburgh	vs. Cincinnati
June 26:	Jackie Brandt, San Francisco	vs. Philadelphia
July 2:	Gene Freese, Philadelphia	vs. Cincinnati
July 5:	Bill White, St. Louis	vs. San Francisco
July 9:	Gene Freese, Philadelphia	vs. St. Louis
July 22:	Earl Averill, Chicago	vs. Los Angeles
July 23:	Willie Jones, Cincinnati	vs. Milwaukee
Aug. 1:	Bob Purkey, Cincinnati	vs. Chicago
Aug. 9:	Ed Bouchee, Philadelphia	vs. St. Louis
Aug. 13:	Alvin Dark, Chicago	vs. San Francisco
Aug. 13:	George Crowe, St. Louis	vs. Los Angeles (pinch hit)
Aug. 13:	Frank Robinson, Cincinnati	vs. Milwaukee
Aug. 29:	Ernie Banks, Chicago	vs. Milwaukee
Sept. 9:	Bobby Avila, Milwaukee	vs. St. Louis
Sept. 19:	Del Crandall, Milwaukee	vs. Philadelphia
Sept. 22:	Hal Smith, St. Louis	vs. Los Angeles

Prolific Outbursts

The biggest one-game outburst of 1959 was, of course, Rocky Colavito's four home runs in one game against Baltimore on June 10. Hitting four homers in one game is one of baseball's rarest feats, but hitting three is not as common as sunrise and sunset either. It is, indeed, one of baseball's special shows.

With baseball laboring through the dead-ball era for the first two decades of this century, it wasn't until 1922 and the third year of the lively ball that anyone pasted three boomers in one game. (For you trivia addicts, it was future umpire Butch Henline for the Phillies in the National League and Ken Williams of the Browns in the American, both in 1922.)

Difficult though the feat is, generally you can expect a few guys each year to get hot and set off multiple bombs in one game. In 1959, it happened twice in the American League and three times in the National.

On May 3, Detroit's Charlie Maxwell homered in his last at-bat in the first game of a doubleheader against the Yankees. Thus warmed up, Charlie proceeded to reach the seats in his first three official at-bats in game two, giving him four homers in four consecutive times at bat. He was the sixth player in major league history to get stuck in so eminent a rut and only the fifth American League player to homer four times in a doubleheader.

The other American Leaguer to take the trot three times in one game that year was Kansas City's Bob Cerv, who did it at home against the Red Sox on August 20. Bob hit his first two in the second and third innings, then "slumped"

111

Detroit's Charlie Maxwell, who had three homers in one game and four in a doubleheader—all hit consecutively. L.

Bob Cerv, Kansas City slugger. R.

until the eighth, when he banged his third. Like 15 of the men who were his teammates at various times during the season, Cerv was an ex-Yankee. And like five others, he was also a future Yankee.

The first National Leaguer to achieve the three-in-a-game feat in 1959 was Don Demeter of the Los Angeles Dodgers, who did it on April 21. Don did it at home at the Los Angeles Coliseum, where the nearby left-field screen was a conniving ally that turned high fly balls into home runs; although Don's first was an inside-the-park shot that went into the Coliseum's more distant regions. Demeter's third home-run of the game came in the eleventh inning and was a game-winner.

On June 21, home run buster Henry Aaron hit three in a game against the Giants in San Francisco. It was the only time in his record-making career that the all-time home-run champ ever popped three in one game.

Also hitting three in one game for the only time in his explosive career was Cincinnati's Frank Robinson, who hit them consecutively against the Cardinals at Cincinnati's Crosley Field on August 22.

There was a curious consistency to the slugging these five men did in their outstanding games: each had no other hits but the home runs, each scored three runs in his game and each drove in six.

In 1958, Dave Philly of the Philadelphia Phillies was the National League pinch-hitting leader, delivering 18 hits in 44 at-bats for a .409 average, which included a record eight-consecutive pinch hits. A year later, he was just as hot, delivering 15 times in 38 pinch-hit opportunities for a .395 average. Another lethal man in the pinch was Ted Williams. Despite a record average of only .254 in 1959, the Red Sox star delivered in eleven of 24 pinch-hitting opportunities for a lusty .458 average.

Five Hits in a Game

In 1959, sixteen players made games look like batting practice, each coming up with five hits. The record for one player doing it in a single season is four, achieved by—and wouldn't you know it—Ty Cobb in 1922 and Stan Musial in 1948. Cobb actually did it three times in a stretch of ten days. In 1959, however, there were no repeaters, with eight different players doing it in each league.

American League

On April 10, Chicago's Nelson Fox had three singles, a double, and a home run (one of two he hit all year) in a 14-inning game against the Tigers. For Nelson, on his way to an MVP year, this was a great send-off.

On April 18, Elston Howard of the Yankees pecked away at the Red Sox with five singles.

On April 21, Cleveland's Minnie Miñoso turned in a nice day's work when he rapped three singles and two homers against the Tigers, driving in six runs.

Washington's Bob Allison had a day for himself on June 5, getting three singles and two home runs against the Tigers. It was the only time during the year, however, that a team with a five-hit man in the lineup lost the game. But Washington did that sort of thing a lot in 1959, as they finished last.

Jim Landis of the White Sox had a double and four singles against the Athletics on July 4.

On August 14, Detroit's Eddie Yost, better known for the many walks he drew, swung the bat steadily and effectively against the Indians, racking up five singles.

On August 23, Detroit's Harvey Kuenn, who was to win the batting championship that year, bore down against the Orioles and went home with four singles and a triple.

Stan Musial, an 18-year veteran in 1959.

On September 10, the Yankees' Mickey Mantle had three singles, a double and a home run against the Athletics.

National League

On April 26, the Dodgers' Charlie Neal peppered the Cardinals with three singles, a double and a triple. This was a 17-11 Dodger win, meaning that Charlie wasn't the only one with his eye on the ball in this game.

On June 21, Pittsburgh's backup-catcher Danny Kravitz had the game of his life against the Cardinals, collect-

Charlie Neal. L.

Cincinnati's Vada Pinson. R.

ing two singles and three doubles. (Danny's average for the season was .253; without that one day's work, it would have been .229.)

Cincinnati's Gus Bell had a big day on July 15, tattooing Cardinal pitching for three singles and two doubles.

On August 6, Pittsburgh's regular catcher, Smoky Burgess, emulated Kravitz by hammering five hits in a game; in Smoky's case it was two singles, two doubles and a home run.

On August 13, the Cubs' George Altman slammed three singles and two home runs against the Giants.

In one of the most lethal two-man batting displays seen in a long time, a pair of Cincinnati stars rapped out ten hits between them during a 15-13 slugfest with the Phillies. The date was August 14 (the same day Eddie Yost had five hits against Cleveland), and dividing those ten hits equally between them were Frank Robinson and Vada Pinson, Cincinnati's scintillating 20-year-old star. In helping their team to a rather busy win, Robinson had three singles, a double, and a home run, while Pinson had three singles and two doubles.

On September 15, the Dodgers' rookie shortstop Maury Wills had four singles and a triple in a 10-inning game against the Milwaukee Braves.

Six hits in a game? That hasn't been done in the American League since 1955 and not in a nine-inning game since 1953; and not in the National League since 1953.

One-Hitters

Of all baseball players, pitchers probably have the longest memories. Conversations with some long-retired gentlemen of the mound reveal them describing the speed, break, and location of specific pitches that may have been delivered fifty or sixty years before. Curiously, failure and defeat are more vividly inscribed upon their memories than success and victory, which, while it may not tell us anything about human nature at large, does allow a glimpse into the often melancholy psyches of certain pitchers.

As a matter of fact, the fraternity at large is frequently maligned by their professional brethren. "Pitchers are prima donnas," "Pitchers are not ballplayers"—these are kinds of sentiments one hears from ballplayers who pride themselves on being multi-talented and playing every day. How these manly fellows are able to adjust to the long-accepted baseball wisdom proclaiming that the non-ballplaying prima donnas are "eighty-five percent of the game" is left to speculation.

So it has been established that pitchers are sensitive and that they have long memories, a combination sure to lead to nightmares and regrets. And for a pitcher, few professional adventures are sulked over longer or with more thumb-sucking gloom than what was, ironically, one of the great moments of his career—a one-hitter.

"I'd much rather pitch a two-hitter than a one-hitter," old-time White Sox ace Ted Lyons once said. "I pitched a one-hitter in the Twenties and I'll never forget it—that one hit. I can still see the pitch going down the pipe and I can still see the bat coming around and making contact. It's one of the most vivid memories of my career, and I think about it more than I do of the no-hitter I pitched."

There were ten one-hitters pitched in the major leagues in 1959, five in each league, some of them quite dramatic.

American League

On May 1, Chicago's Early Wynn beat the Red Sox, 1-0, on a one-hitter, the hit being a first-inning single by Pete Runnels. The 39-year-old Wynn also pitched a couple of two-hitters later in the season.

Hoyt Wilhelm, the Baltimore knuckleballer who had no-hit the Yankees the year before, almost did it again on May 22. In shutting out the New Yorkers, Wilhelm allowed only an eighth-inning single by Jerry Lumpe.

Chicago's Billy Pierce, who once was deprived of a perfect game by a bloop hit with two out in the ninth, pitched a one-hitter against the Washington Senators on June 11. Ron Samford's double in the third inning was the lone hit.

On July 4, the Yankees' Bob Turley came painfully close to entering the pitchers' dream world. Bullet Bob had no-hit the Senators for eight innings, when Julio Becquer led off the ninth inning with the only hit the Senators would get. Turley also had a pair of two-hitters that year.

Washington's Camilo Pascual pitched a five-inning one-hitter against Detroit on July 15, Gus Zernial getting the only hit.

National League

Philadelphia's Rookie of the Year Jack Sanford fired a one-hitter against the St. Louis Cardinals on April 18, with a single by Stan Musial in the seventh inning breaking it up.

Sanford wasn't alone in feeling this particular sting of the Musial bat in 1959, for three days later the Cubs' Glen Hobbie was working on a no-hitter when up came Musial in the seventh inning and whacked a double.

On May 26, there was the famous Harvey Haddix 12-

Billy Pierce, White Sox left-hander.   *L.*

Bob Turley of the New York Yankees.   *R.*

perfect-innings game, which ended with Harvey losing a 13-inning one-hitter (the game is covered in detail earlier in this book).

On June 21, Chicago right-hander John Buzhardt one-hit the Phillies, the lone hit a single by Carl Sawatski in the third inning. It was Buzhardt's only complete game in ten starts.

On June 30, San Francisco's Sam Jones pitched a one-hitter against the Dodgers, the only hit coming with two out in the eighth, when Jim Gilliam outlegged a scratch hit to the infield. The hit was controversial—Giant shortstop Andre Rodgers did not play the ball cleanly—but the scorer ruled that Gilliam would have beat it out anyway. This was a pretty stiff-backed call, considering that Jones had a no-hitter going, with two out in the eighth.

Career Interruption Codes

AA	—	Injured in automobile accident
AJ	—	Arm injury
AL	—	Alcohol problem
BA	—	Broken arm
BC	—	Broken or dislocated collarbone
BE	—	Broken bone in elbow
BF	—	Broken bone in foot
BG	—	Broken finger
BH	—	Broken bone in hand
BJ	—	Broken jaw
BK	—	Broken bone in knee
BL	—	Broken leg
BN	—	Broken ankle
BP	—	Broken hipbone
BR	—	Broken rib or ribs
BS	—	Broken bone in shoulder
BT	—	Broken toe
BW	—	Broken wrist
BX	—	Broken spine
BY	—	Broken cheekbone
BZ	—	Broken nose
CJ	—	Face injury
CN	—	Concussion
CP	—	Blood poisoning
DD	—	Died during the season or the following off-season
DE	—	Declared ineligible by commissioner or league president
DL	—	Declared ineligible for life by commissioner
DO	—	Declared ineligible for playing in outlaw league
DP	—	On team for entire year–but did not play
DR	—	Drug problem
DU	—	Unofficially declared ineligible for life
EJ	—	Elbow injury
FA	—	Finger amputated
FJ	—	Foot or heel injury
FR	—	Badly burned
FS	—	Fractured skull
GJ	—	Groin injury
GW	—	Gunshot wounds
HJ	—	Hand injury
HO	—	Holdout
IF	—	Didn't play in order to be with a member of the family who was ill
IJ	—	Eye injury
IL	—	Illness
IN	—	Couldn't play because of injunction

		issued by Pennsylvania Court in suit brought by Phi. NL
JA	—	In jail for assault
JJ	—	Injury or on disabled list—type of injury unknown
JL	—	Went to play in Japanese League
JT	—	Jumped team
KB	—	Killed by pitched ball
KJ	—	Knee injury
KP	—	Kept out of lineup as part of A.L.-N.L. peace agreement in 1903
LA	—	Leg amputated
LJ	—	Leg or thigh injury—including achilles tendon
ML	—	Special military leave to play baseball
MM	—	Merchant marine
MS	—	Military service
NJ	—	Ankle injury
PB	—	Head injury from pitched ball
PJ	—	Hip injury
QJ	—	Brain injury
RC	—	Retired to coach
RJ	—	Finger injury
RL	—	Reported late in order to finish school year or returned to school before the end of the baseball season
RM	—	Retired to manage
RP	—	Attended to personal business
RR	—	Refused to report
SA	—	Sore arm
SC	—	Barred by court injunction
SD	—	Suspended by commissioner for drug use
SJ	—	Shoulder injury or shoulder separation
SL	—	Suspended by commissioner or league president
SM	—	Suspended for playing in the Mexican League
ST	—	Suspended by team
SU	—	Suspended for hitting or abusing umpire
TJ	—	Chest injury
UJ	—	Side injury
VJ	—	Rib injury
VR	—	Voluntarily retired
WJ	—	Wrist injury
WW	—	Voluntarily retired or played only part-time while working for the government or in plants producing war material
XJ	—	Back injury
YJ	—	Head injury
ZJ	—	Neck injury

121

About the Author

Don Honig is one of America's best-known and prolific baseball historians. He is the author of 25 books about the national pastime, including *Baseball When the Grass Was Real*, *Baseball Between the Lines*, *Baseball America*, plus histories of the National League, the American League, the World Series, the All-Star Game, the New York Yankees, the New York Mets and the Los Angeles Dodgers. Mr. Honig is also the author of *The Donald Honig Reader* and has written over 30 baseball titles for young readers. He lives in Cromwell, Connecticut.